Stand By Yer Beds!

Memories of
National Service
in the
Royal Air Force
1947 to 1962

John F. Hamlin

First published 1995
by GMS Enterprises
67 Pyhill, Bretton
Peterborough
England
PE3 8QQ

Tel & Fax 01733-265123

Copyright: John F. Hamlin

ISBN 1 870384 41 5

The main text of this book
has been set in 10pt 'Times'
on an Apple Macintosh DTP system

Printed and bound by
GMS Enterprises

CONTENTS

Personal Reminiscences

Appendix

Apart from tendering my sincere thanks to all those former National Servicemen who responded to my appeals, whether or not I used their contributions in this book, I wish to thank Mr. Charles Hall ('Holly') for drawing the cartoons which illustrate some of the anecdotes and also the front cover.

ABBREVIATIONS

AC1	Aircraftman First Class	NAAFI	Navy, Army & Air Force Institute
AC2	Aircraftman Second Class	NATO	North Atlantic Treaty Organisation
AFS	Advanced Flying School	NCO	Non-commissioned Officer
AFTS	Advanced Flying Training School	NS	National Service
AOC	Air Officer Commanding	OCU	Operational Conversion Unit
ATC	Air Training Corps	PA	Personal assistant
AVTAG	(aviation fuel)	Plt. Off.	Pilot Officer
BFTS	Basic Flying Training School	POR	Personnel Occurrence Report
CCF	Combined Cadet Force	PT	Physical training
CO	Commanding Officer	RAFVR	RAF Volunteer Reserve
Cpl.	Corporal	RCAF	Royal Canadian Air Force
Flg. Off.	Flying Officer	RU	Reception Unit
Flt. Lt.	Flight Lieutenant	R/T	Radio telephone
Flt. Sgt.	Flight Sergeant	SAC	Senior Aircraftman
FTS	Flying Training School	SD	Special Duties
GCI	Ground Controlled Interception	Sgt.	Sergeant
GD	General Duties (i.e. aircrew)	SNCO	Senior Non-commissioned Officer
GEE	(a form of radar)	SoRT	School of Recruit Training
Gp. Capt.	Group Captain	SoTT	School of Technical Training
J/T	Junior Technocian	Sqdn. Ldr.	Squadron Leader
KD	Khaki Drill (clothing)	SRO	Station Routine Orders
LAA	Light Anti-aircraft	USAF	United States Air Force
LAC	Leading Aircraftman	u/t	untrained or under training
MEAF	Middle East Air Force	Wg. Cdr.	Wing Commander
MI	Medical Inspection	WRAF	Women's Royal Air Force
MT	Motor Transport	Wt. Off.	Warrant Officer
MU	Maintenance Unit		

INTRODUCTION

It is now many years since conscription of young men into the armed forces after the Second World War was a part of everyday life. Those who were taken in to the three services at eighteen years of age, whether they wanted to be taken or not, are now anything up to 66 years of age, and very little has been written to place the events which befell them on record. Until entering the Forces, many of the recruits had never been away from home, but they had to become accustomed very quickly to the highly disciplined, intensive training common to all three services. Most benefited greatly from the arduous recruit training; physically, many had never been so fit before (or since!), and most were imbued with new-found self-confidence. And what of the considerable difference in the backgrounds and academic abilities of the National Servicemen? In the 'pit' next to yours on one side might be a University maths graduate; on the other side a builder's labourer. You didn't find such a widespread difference among the regulars!

This volume is an attempt by one who is proud to have been a National Serviceman in the Royal Air Force to record the service lives of a number of men who were kind enough to respond to appeals he made. By far the greater number of respondents stated that, in retrospect, while they may have 'binded' as much as anyone at the time, they acquired a great deal of experience of life during their service, for which they are grateful. A few were unlucky in that the authorities did not see fit to give them work for which they were most suited, but others were trained in occupations which stood them in good stead later. Several letters came from men who consider that the present generation are the unlucky ones in not having the chance to enjoy the opportunities that we did.

There was considerable mention, in the letters I received, of the dreaded drill instructors who made our lives a misery during recruit training, but all admit that most of these men were doing a difficult job in converting a couple of dozen callow youths into smart, self-disciplined young men in eight weeks. Underneath the bluster, most of the DIs were as proud of the recruits on passing-out parades as the recruits were themselves. DIs were extremely smart, with boots polished to perfection and with creases like razors in their battledress trousers, in which some of them placed chains to hold the trouser-legs over the tops of their gaiters. Remember how they clanked as they walked? Like everyone, they had a job to do and in general they did it well.

Trades in which NS men found themselves were many and varied, from clerks of different varieties through air traffic control assistants and cooks to the technical trades — radio, airframe and engine mechanics, to name a few. By being taught these occupations, many young men were able to place a foot on the ladder up which they would climb after returning to civilian life. Few National Servicemen were trained as pilots or navigators, but of the small number many were able to go on to greater things, either by signing on to make the RAF their careers or by taking employment in similar work with civilian airlines. Had they not had this opportunity, few would have been able, for reasons of finance, to pursue a career in aviation.

Little information is to hand about the number of National Servicemen who took the plunge and signed on for further service, but anecdotal evidence suggests that many seriously considered the option of rejoining after finding it difficult to settle down in 'Civvie Street'. I was one such young man! Several correspondents have pondered on 'what might have been' had they signed on — such was the effect that time spent in the Service had on people. My personal feeling is that no other period of my life had such a long-lasting and indeed beneficial influence on me.

I have compiled this book in an attempt to place on record some of the facts behind National Service in the Royal Air Force, but more particularly to provide the personal histories of a number of kind people who helped me fulfil a long-standing desire to tell the story of a large group of young men whose valuable service might otherwise be forgotten. My intention was to include each letter verbatim, but in the end I decided to edit many of them slightly in order to keep the book to a reasonable size! I have tried, however, to retain the correspondents' own words as far as possible and have certainly not altered the spirit of their letters.

John F. Hamlin
Newmarket
July 1995

INTENTIONALLY BLANK

THE HISTORY OF NATIONAL SERVICE IN THE POSTWAR ROYAL AIR FORCE

Post-war National Service in all three Armed Forces, already effectively in operation as a continuation of what had been known as the Duration Of The Present Emergency, was regularised by the National Service Act of 18 July 1947. Under this Act, every male British subject aged 18 to 26 (30 for medical and dental professionals) normally resident in the UK was liable to be called upon to serve in the Armed Forces for two terms — 12 months full-time and a period of part time service sixty days in total or 21 days in any one year. The serviceman could opt to enter the Royal Auxiliary Air Force in lieu of this reserve service. A proviso of the 1947 Act was that it would expire at the end of 1953 unless His Majesty the King decided to extend the provisions of the Act.

The National Service Act 1947 was due to come into force on 1 January 1949, but before then a further Act, dated 30 July 1948, was passed as an addendum. This Act confirmed that it was the duty of the Services to provide, as far as practicable,

further education facilities for full-time National Servicemen; to safeguard a man's previous employment by compelling his employer to take him back into the occupation which he had left; and to ensure that a man could not be dismissed by virtue of his annual reserve obligations. Later in 1948, on 16 December, the National Service (Amendment) Act was passed to increase the period of full-time service from 12 to 18 months, with three years' part-time obligation.

The 18-month period of service was in force only until 1 October 1950, when, due to the outbreak of the Korean War and the possibility of world conflict, it became mandatory to serve two years. It was probably at this time that the scope of National Service became open-ended, the original 31 December 1953 deadline being scrapped. So for the remainder of the National Service scheme the two-year period of service was the norm.

By 1955, it became clear that the need for large numbers of recruits to the RAF (and indeed the other services) was declining, and from that time the intake diminished each year. A 'White Paper' approved on 17 April 1957 outlined radical changes in defence policy and a progressive reduction in National Service intakes, ending at the end of 1960. Over six months from April that year, National Service intake actually increased by 1500 men, forcing the period of basic training to be reduced to seven weeks. Eventually it was decided that the 'threshold' date of birth which would determine whether a young man would carry out National Service or not would be 30 September 1939; if he

Get Some In!

RAF STRENGTHS 1957 - 1962

The table below illustrates the decline in numbers of both the National Service and the regular elements of the Royal Air Force, and the relatively faster reduction in numbers of National Servicemen compared with regulars.

Date	Nat. Service	Regular	Total	% of regular
1.4.57 (actual)	68700	153900	222600	30.86
1.4.58 (estimate)	46700	141300	188000	24.84
1.4.59 (actual)	26500	142300	168800	15.70
1.4.60 (estimate)	18400	139400	157800	11.66
1.4.61 (actual)	13400	131800	145200	9.23
1.4.62 (estimate)	5400	128900	134300	4.02

was born on or after 1 October 1939 he would not be required, much to the chagrin of those with birthdays just before that date! However, in order to sweep up a large number of people who had either not been called up on their expected dates due to a temporary surplus of recruits or who had been deferred on grounds of apprenticeship, for example, intake continued for over three more years, until the last week of January 1961. According to official records, the last service number to be issued to a National Serviceman during the final official intake of fifty recruits, in the third week of November 1960, was 5082226, which applied to one AC2 Farrer. Most of these men were 'deferments' aged up to 21 years six months old. However, it appears that a few men were inducted in December 1960 and January 1961, but these may have had their service numbers being pre-allocated. At the same time some men were being released up to six months early. The very last National Serviceman to be demobilised is said to have been SAC Joe Wallace, who left RAF Kinloss on 23 January 1963 in a Shackleton aircraft bound for his home town, Glasgow.

So ended the fourteen-year period of post-war conscription into the Royal Air Force, during which nearly half a million men had passed through the portals of the two Reception Units. Whatever may be said about the scheme, it has never been doubted that without these men, who worked in most, if not all, trades and at Stations worldwide, the RAF would not have been able to meet the demands put upon it.

In choosing the personal accounts to include in Chapter 2, it has been difficult to decide the starting point. In the end, January 1947 was selected, as that was when the two major batches of service numbers specifically allocated to National Servicemen came into use. The fact that the Act of Parliament laying down the post-war criteria did not come into force until some time later has been regarded as irrelevant, as conscription had continued almost unabated since the end of the War.

RECEPTION UNITS

1 Reception Unit, RAF Padgate

This unit, known to huge numbers of recruits, both National Service and Regular, during wartime and early post-war years, was situated near Warrington in Lancashire and shared the site with 3 School of Recruit Training. During the early 1950s, an average of 1000 recruits arrived at 1 RU each week for kitting out and induction before being sent to any one of a number of Schools of Recruit Training. By the autumn of 1952, intake figures were declining, and 1 RU finally closed on 15 June 1953, from which date all airman entrants to the RAF were dealt with at 2 RU, RAF Cardington.

2 Reception Unit, RAF Cardington

Until 1 RU closed in June 1953, 2 RU at RAF Cardington, near Bedford, had processed mainly regular recruits. From that time, however, National Servicemen arrived at the average rate of 3000 per month, dropping slightly to less than 2800 in 1954 and increasing to 3500 per month in 1955, all less any recruits who dropped out on medical or other grounds. Reliable figures for the last years are not available from unit records, but the statistics given in another part of this Chapter will give an indication of the numbers of men involved, all of whom passed through 2 RU. Towards the end, 867 men reported to 2 RU in October 1960, 368 in November (of whom 5082226 AC2 Farrer was one), and 9 in December, who remain something of a mystery, as do the 19 in January 1961.

The total number of National Service recruits dealt with at 2 RU between January 1949 and 30 November 1960 was 385,565, an average of approximately 2700 per month. 2 RU closed on 6 February 1961, having processed the final handful of recruits, and from that date all reception of regular recruits was handled at RAF Bridgnorth.

SCHOOLS OF RECRUIT TRAINING

which trained National Servicemen

3 School of Recruit Training, RAF Padgate

Located on the same Station as 1 Reception Unit, 3 SoRT, retitled from 3 Recruit Centre in March 1950, dealt with both regular and National Service recruits until the final intake at the end of 1956. The final passing-out parade was held on 24 January 1957, and the unit closed down a week later.

4 School of Recruit Training, RAF Wilmslow.

Perhaps better known as the WRAF training station, RAF Wilmslow, near Manchester, was also the home of 4 SoRT until 20 November 1959, when the final group of recruits passed out. In March 1953 Wilmslow had played host to thousands of recruits from other Schools who gathered there for intensive drill practice before taking part in the RAF's 35th birthday parade, held in Manchester.

5 School of Recruit Training, RAF West Kirby.

Known to many recruits as a place best avoided, West Kirby, on the Wirral peninsula, seems to have trained more National Service recruits than any other School of Recruit Training. The Station had been used for this purpose since 1946, and before long 5 SoRT was specialising in conscripts. Being quite close to the mountains of North Wales, 5 SoRT sent its recruits there for 'initiative training', an event not forgotten many years later by those involved! Intake 39, which entered 5 SoRT on 25 October 1957, was the final one, and passed out on 20 December 1957, the Station then closing.

6 School of Recruit Training, RAF Credenhill.

This unit, located just outside Hereford, was training National Service recruits in 1951, but the final passing-out parade was held on 14 February 1952 and the unit then closed.

7 School of Recruit Training, RAF Bridgnorth.

7 SoRT was the last unit to train National Service recruits and was generally regarded as a reasonable place to 'bash the square'. This unit, which had been known as 7 RC until November 1948, appears to have been the one which dealt with the 'bulge' of recruits in the summer of 1960. The last intake, on 16 December 1960, included only four National Servicemen, who passed out at the end of February 1961. 7 SoRT then concentrated on training regulars and on acting as a Reception Centre.

8 School of Recruit Training, RAF Kirkham.

One of the earlier Schools, 8 SoRT was active only until 75B Flight recruits held their passing-out parade on 16 May 1952, after which the unit disbanded.

STATISTICS

Detailed statistics for the early part of the National Service scheme are sparse, but by 1950 the official figures were given some substance by the breaking-down of the annual total intake into categories. In total, the number of young men who were conscripted from 1947 to 1961 inclusive was 433087 (probably including rejects), made up as follows:

Year	Officers			Aircrew	Airmen Ground	Total	Total
	GD	Non-GD	Total				
1947							48031
1948							46952
1949			350			43166	43516
1950	14	352	366	5	52148	52153	52519
1951	10	246	256		47206	47206	47462
1952	14	442	456		39356	39356	39812
1953	36	250	286		36550	36550	36836
1954	56	251	307		33288	33288	33595
1955	58	173	231		41953	41953	42184
1956	64	149	213		36560	36560	36773
1957	4	146	150	6	20655	20661	20811
1958	2	125	127		12018	12018	12145
1959	2	188	190		11128	11128	11318
1960	1	92	93		9051	9051	9144
1961		1	1		19	19	20
TOTAL	261	2415	3026	11	339932	383109	433087

SERVICE NUMBERS

Service numbers allocated to National Service personnel were as follows:

Service number batch	Dates of allocation	Quantity	Remarks
2340000 — 2599999	1.47 - 7.53	260,000	Non-ATC
2700000 — 2787999	7.53 - 2.56	88,000	Non-ATC
3100000 — 3156537**	5.49 - c.57	56,538	Ex-ATC
5010251 — 5010916	2.56 - ?	666	Non-ATC
5010917 — 5012250**	5.56 - ?	1334	Ex-CCF (RAF)
5012251 — 5012999	2.56 - 11.60	749	Non-ATC granted postponement
5013000 — 5082226	2.56 - 11.60	69,227	Non -ATC
5090000 — 5099999	5.57?	10,000	Granted postponement
5100000 — 5100357**	2.59 - ?	358	Ex-CCF (RAF)
5190000 — 5194999	1.57 - ?	5000	Aircrew

** signifies ex ATC or CCF (RAF) recruit

9 School of Recruit Training, RAF Weeton.

Handling mainly National Servicemen, 9 SoRT had an average intake of 100 men per week in 1951, up to 1000 recruits being under training at any one time. The final parade was held on 3 July 1952, and remaining recruits were transferred to 3 SoRT.

10 School of Recruit Training, RAF Melksham.

Better known as the home of a School of Technical Training, RAF Melksham also housed 10 SoRT. In January 1951 the average weekly intake was about 100, most of whom were National Servicemen. A final intake arrived in June 1953 and passed out on 17 August, and the unit closed a week later.

11 School of Recruit Training, Hednesford

By the early 1950s, 11 SoRT was accepting an average weekly intake of 350 men, not all of them National Servicemen. On 24 September 1952, Intake 92 arrived, comprising 367 National Service recruits, all of whom were POMs (Potential Officer Material) — this was the first, and possibly only, complete intake of such men.

Due to an urgent demand for accommodation for Hungarian refugees, a closing date for 11 SoRT was brought forward, and after the passing-out parade of Intake 36 on 3 December 1956 the unit closed and vacated the Station by 21 December.

13 School of Recruit Training, RAF Innsworth.

Opened in September 1950, 13 SoRT handled some National Servicemen, the combined average weekly intake being about 100. The School made a name for itself in March 1952 by persuading over 5% of the NS recruits there to sign on as regulars, the highest figure so far. However, the final passing-out parade was held on 14 November 1952 and the unit then closed down.

PERSONAL REMINISCENCES

There follows a number of accounts, received by the author in the form of letters, some of which have been edited to a greater or lesser degree and one or two censored! For providing so readily information on their experiences, my sincere thanks go the gentleman named at the head of each letter. To those whose letters have not been included, my thanks are given nevertheless.

❏ Mr. Brian P. Mears (3100917)

I was in the ATC and was called up in January 1947. I was called to RAF Padgate for uniform and IQ tests and it was decided to train me as a radar mechanic. In January 1947 it was cold, and I remember standing on a folded newspaper to keep my feet from freezing in the new heavy black boots!

Then I went square-bashing at RAF West Kirby for a few weeks. While I was there the camp froze up and most of us in Hut C14 of 19 Flight were given two weeks' leave, marching away through dark country roads to the railway station to catch our trains.

After a pleasant two weeks at home there was an announcement on the radio — "All recruits due back At West Kirby are granted a further two weeks leave and ration books, warrants, etc. will be posted to you". So I spent two more weeks in Bedford, with the snow melting, causing the River Ouse to break its banks.

At last back to West Kirby and a feeling of fitness after six more weeks of drill in the damp cold air and the smell of the coal smoke from the billet stoves! Our drill instructor was Cpl. Timpson, and all the instructors were very smart.

Then in March or April 1947 I was posted to RAF West Malling in Kent, which was surrounded by cherry orchards. There I spent six months of nice hot summer in the Radar Section, where A.I. radar was serviced. While there I carried out some night guard duties in the orchards and some summer mornings skiving in an old Anson! After this I was posted to RAF Yatesbury for a 30-week radar course. The exercise books which we filled up with notes were marked Secret! When I completed the course I was posted to RAF Debden, a well-built camp with brick-built billets on two floors, and with hangars and other buildings built to last fifty years. Most of the time we spent dismantling old Japanese radar and radio gear, and we had one of the first wire recorders, as opposed to tape. The Warrant Officer was called "Sticky" Marsh.

The old bomb dump at Debden was full of old radio and radar gear, and some of my friends used to build TV sets from the dismantled parts. Several of us had motor-bikes, and speed trials were held some lunch-times and evenings on a disused runway. Some petrol had been found in the wing tanks of a hangared Halifax aircraft, which had convenient drain taps!

After a pleasant summer at Debden I was posted to Coleraine, Northern Ireland, where I lived in a civilian billet (Mrs. Snodland was the landlady) three miles from a radar station we were decommissioning. My demob was held up for a while due to the Berlin airlift, but eventually I joined 'G' Reserve and eighteen months after being 'demobbed' I spent a good two-week 'holiday' at Swingate, near Dover, with a new uniform.

❏ Dr. James D. Jones (2340652)

January 1947, the month in which I joined the RAF at Padgate, saw the start of one of the worst winters this century, and after kitting out was sent to 5 RCU at RAF Innsworth, just outside Gloucester. The camp ran out of solid fuel for the hut stoves, so the recruits were issued with railway passes and were told to go home and the camp was closed. Every week I received a telegram giving me a further seven days leave and a postal order for £1-8-0 (£1.40), plus extra money for 'lodging allowance'. When the snow melted the River Severn flooded the city of Gloucester, whose residents were evacuated to Innsworth camp, thus prolonging my home leave. Most of my parents' friends assumed that I had been invalided out of the RAF!

Some weeks after Easter, over four months after joining the RAF, I was recalled to Insworth, where I completed recruit training. I opted for the trade of Medical Orderly and was posted to RAF Marsworth, near Tring in Hertfordshire. Marsworth was on the site of a disused airfield [Cheddington-Ed.], and the Nissen hut accommodation was scattered over several dispersed sites in beautiful countryside on the banks of the Grand Union Canal. In contrast to the winter, the summer of 1947 was very hot. London was only a short journey away so that we could go there on weekend passes. Most sports were played, and the Captain of the cricket team and producer of the Station Dramatic Society was Cpl. Brian Rix, now Lord Rix.

I was 'passed out' as an AC1 medical orderly and posted to RAF West Kirby. This was a 'dream' posting, as my parents' home was only a mile from the main gate! I worked in various sections of the busy hospital, which looked after the health of four recruit training Wings. I was elevated to the rank of LAC and looked forward to spending the rest of my National Service there. But this was not to be, as in early 1948 I was posted to the Middle East via RAF Burtonwood, where I was kitted out in the usual KD.

Suitably equipped, I travelled to Southampton to board the Orient Line troopship *SS Otranto*. I spent about five weeks in a hammock while we toured the Mediterranean, including calls at Athens and Salonika. I remember being hungry all the time; catering was by the Army, and they did not like feeding the few RAF men on board! Eventually we disembarked at Port Said, and joined a train which followed the Great Bitter Lakes to RAF El Hamra. This tented camp, known to all Middle East-based airmen, was the transit or movement control Station

HOLLY

for the area. After being in limbo for several weeks, I found myself posted to the permanent staff at El Hamra.

Seeking further promotion, I remustered from the Medical Branch to become a Sergeant in the Education Branch. I attended a teachers' training course at RAF Ismailia, on the banks of the Suez Canal, and then returned to El Hamra to take charge of the Education Section, where I attempted, without much success, to teach colloquial Arabic to uninterested sections of RAF personnel. My year at El Hamra and various neighbouring Stations was a very happy one. We worked only in the mornings, and took part in various sports, mainly swimming and sailing, in the afternoons, although some afternoons were spent sleeping in our tents! At night we usually visited the Station cinema.

I had always hoped that the four months wasted time during my recruit training would not affect my demobilisation, but this was not to be, as the Berlin airlift intervened, delaying all discharges. However, my return from the Middle East was speeded up when I was invited by various University interview Boards to attend for appraisal. Ironically, although I had been in the RAF for over two years, the first RAF aircraft I ever saw at close quarters was the York which flew me to Heathrow via Tripoli. On arrival I made a quick visit to RAF Uxbridge, then went home, before going to RAF Hednesford to be 'de-kitted'. After a week's leave I was 'demobbed' at RAF Warton in May 1949.

Of the sixty males in my subsequent year of medical study at University half were former National Servicemen, who all agreed what a wonderful 'finishing school' it had been. I am sure we all made better doctors for having such an experience.

❑ Mr. David C. Willis (2341607)

Having received my call-up papers, I travelled to RAF Padgate on 14 January 1947 for induction. After a few days of being pushed around we were kitted out and sent to RAF West Kirby, on the frozen Wirral peninsula. Many of us mollicoddled young men soon became aware of another breed — the sadistic permanent staff of square-bashing camps, mostly RAF Regiment types, it seems.

The toughening-up process began and a sort of camaraderie developed amongst the mish-mash thrown together. However, the hardship became more acceptable once the end was in sight and one was able to shout "You'll be sorreee!" to new entrants arriving at camp! Fairly early on, we were taken on a five-mile run without much preparation training. Next morning, my pal and I found it difficult to get out of bed and almost impossible to do more than creep about due to agonisingly stiff thigh muscles. Instead of suffering to work out the stiffness on a second run, we hid in the latrines until the PE group moved off. Needless to say, we were caught, charged and given fourteen days' 'jankers'! So on top of the normal square-bashing daily routine were added defaulters' parades with full pack — early in the morning, at lunchtime, teatime and last thing at night — together with a couple of hours fatigue duty in the evening. One of the duties included climbing above the ovens in the Sergeants' mess kitchen and cleaning the hot black chimneys with melted fat. This was the closest thing to Hades I'd experienced!

January 1947 is on record as a particularly severe period of weather, and as the whole camp froze up we were sent home due to the lack of fuel. We were of course overjoyed to receive unexpected leave in which to relax and nurse our chillblains. After a few days at home I found that I had contracted mumps and was therefore given a further three weeks' medical leave. When I eventually returned to West Kirby I was re-Flighted and had to start again - but I was more experienced this time!

Eventually Passing Out arrived - what pride and happiness! (Don't we all still hold our heads high when we hear the RAF March Past?). I was posted to RAF West Raynham in Norfolk (Fighter Command) to train as a photographer, and things became a lot more interesting and civilised. After my course I was sent to 41 Squadron at RAF Church Fenton in Yorkshire, where I spent the rest of my two-and-a-quarter years. Being a photographer was quite a 'jammy' job, quite often privileged. On top of that I bluffed my way into playing string bass in the Station dance band. Altogether, the period at Church Fenton was a very happy one, and made up for the miseries of West Kirby. However, I'm convinved that the youth of today would benefit, as I did, from the experience.

❑ Mr. James Lowe (3105042)

On 26 January 1947 I reported to RAF Padgate for kitting-out, and remained there to do my basic training. From there I went to 3 Radio School at RAF Compton Bassett, Wiltshire, to be trained as a wireless and teleprinter operator. Having passed out from there I was posted to RAF Honington in Suffolk, which was at that time a Major Servicing Unit in Transport Command. This was at the time of the Berlin airlift and the Station was working flat out servicing aircraft engaged in this operation and also

flying spares out to Wunstorf and Gatow in Germany. This involved loading Dakotas, Yorks and Hastings with spare engines etc. No matter what trade, everyone became loaders, working shift work around the clock, and I found it the hardest manual work I have ever done in my life. During that hot Suffolk summer we were grateful for the odd crate of beer generously given to us by some of the aircrews.

From Honington I was sent to the Far East, sailing on the *MV Dilwara* for Singapore, a five-week voyage. On arrival I went to work at the Singapore Signals Centre at RAF Changi, receiving endless 'bandit' reports from 'up-country' Malaya`. This was at the time of the Malayan emergency (Operation 'Firedog'), and unfortunately two of my colleagues lost their lives while there. We were also in contact with Royal Navy ships on the China Station, including *HMS Amethyst, Black Swan* and *Cossack,* which were trapped in the Yangste River by the Chinese communists about that time.

While I was at Changi I became very friendly with Charles Calman, a former air gunner from Dundee who was by then an LAC MT driver. I met him again in 1993 for the first time for 45 years — quite a reunion, as you can imagine.

I was finally demobbed on 16 August 1949 after a very interesting and eventful National Service, and I am proud to think that but for this period of service I would not have been able to take part in events which are part of this country's military history.

❑ Mr. G. W. Cooke (3103777)

At sixteen years of age I joined the Air Training Corps (204 Sqdn.), which I attended once a week and enjoyed. The idea of joining was to get into the RAF, the best way since there was no shortage of manpower at the time. One Saturday in 1947 my call-up papers were delivered, telling me to report to RAF Padgate on a certain date. I said goodbye to the people at the Post Office where I worked as a messenger boy, but the hardest to say goodbye to was my mother, as I was the third son to join the RAF and she was left without a son in the house to do the odd jobs.

I boarded the train at Lincoln for the long journey to Padgate, from where some RAF transport took us to the camp gates. A Sergeant took us to the cookhouse, a long building just like a British Restaurant, which we had all been used to during the war. After the meal, which was very good, the Sergeant took us to the blanket store, where we were issued with three blankets and a pillow, and we then trooped along the road for some distance until we came to a number of Nissen huts. It had been a long day, and I was soon asleep.

Next day after breakfast we were given a talk on what to expect during the next few days and then were marched to the clothing store for kitting-out. An uninterested WAAF asked my chest size and then gave me a greatcoat which looked big enough for two people. Next, two pairs of trousers (one for working and for best), a battle-dress tunic, a best blue tunic, a khaki battle-dress and so on until I had a kitbag full of all I would need to be a properly dressed airman at all times.

After our visit to the clothing store we were told that we had been posted to Padgate for our basic training. Talking among ourselves, we came to the conclusion that we'd rather be sent to a place we knew than travel to a place we didn't know. So we were lined up and marched to our 'square-bashing' camp, which was part of Padgate but far enough from the new recruits for them not to hear what was going on. I was a member of 'C' Flight, Intake 109. We all found a bed and sat on it, but not for long, as in came one of the smartest airmen I had ever seen. He was not dressed in blue, but wore an army uniform with an RAF hat, and also had gaiters. He was a Corporal DI, the worst type of creature in the RAF! This man was a tall chap, and turned out to be fair in most things. He lived in a room at the end of the Nissen hut so that he could be on hand at all times. Later, he told us what was expected, how the blues were to be folded, the beds made up, boots cleaned, and above all, how to keep the room in top condition. Before he left he asked who would like to be Senior Man in the hut; one man spoke up, saying that he had been in the RAF before but had been sick for a number of months, and knew what was expected. The rest of us heaved a sigh of relief!

A new day dawned, and we were lined up for inspection. An officer came to give us a talk about the training, the first officer we had seen. He was a nice chap, well spoken, and told us that if we had any problems we should ask for his advice. That was the last we ever saw of him! The next person to speak was a Sergeant, but his talk and his language were so awful they are best forgotten. If he wanted to put the fear of God into us he succeeded with a vengeance. He too was a very smart chap, who we could not help admiring for his turnout. Our hut's Senior Man told us how to clean boots with a toothbrush, beating the toecaps with the brush until they shone. The stove in the middle of the room was everyone's concern, and had to be cleaned daily with black lead polish.

The days went by slowly, the routine being - rise, wash, shave, breakfast, toilet, make bed, dress in fatigues, parade outside for inspection. Each airman had to be checked in detail for cleanliness. If a fault was found there was extra work at the end of the day, usually digging the garden outside the hut, which was very hard after a day's work. The day would roll slowly by, with fieldcraft, drill, rifle practice, assault course, route marching and PT (which I hated). We looked forward to the NAAFI breaks - a sit down and a bun was a real treat.

One day when we returned to the hut after a long day which had included a gruelling route march, I was greeted by the sight of my bed covered with kit. The inspecting officer must have found fault with my layout, and soon the Corporal gave out the names of all the airmen who were likewise affected. We had to report to the guardroom for extra duty - no NAAFI that night! After three hours extra work, we had to clean all our gear, and it was then too late to go anywhere, so I curled up on my bed and thought of home and all I had left behind. A very sad person indeed I felt!

In drill I think I got away with quite a lot as I was tall and was picked as right marker. This entailed marching onto the parade ground first so that the rest of the Flight could assemble in threes on me. I was rather proud of being picked, and the DIs never had to tell me off, in fact I had to demonstrate some of the movements. My Flight was picked to provide a guard of honour during an inspection by an Air Commodore, who seemed pleased with the result of the DIs' training in so short a time. Later the Air Commodore ordered me to step forward and asked me how tall I was and whether I was enjoying my time at Padgate. I told him that some aspects of it were enjoyable, but I would be pleased when I could perform the job I had joined the RAF to do, hopefully a driver. He wished me luck and I returned to the ranks.

At last we were allowed our first 48-hour pass, but in the day or two before we were released we were threatened with cancellations, one after another, if we did not come up to scratch with our training. On the Friday the hut was a hive of activity, and we all had to be inspected before we left for home.

The second half of basic training passed much like the first part, until eventually the day of the passing-out parade arrived. Again I was right marker; the Flights formed up, taking their dressing from me, and we marched to the music, up and down, in threes and fours, to all the drills we had practiced over the weeks. We were smart, and it was a pleasure to watch. At the end, the band played the RAF March Past and the Air Commodore took the salute. What a lot of shouting there was when we were back in the hut! It was over, and we could get on with the jobs we had joined the RAF to do.

During training, we had been interviewed to determine which trade we were to be placed in. I had put down as first choice MT Driver, second choice Telephonist, and third Clerk/GD. In the event, I was told that I would be a Clerk/GD if I passed a six-week course, prior to which I was to be posted to RAF Hospital, Cosford to gain practical experience. So that is where I went, in full kit (which I later found was not necessary), and reported for duty. Under the guidance of another airman, I soon learned the work, which I found most interesting. Meals at Cosford were very good, and in the summer weather I really enjoyed the place. We all avoided the main camp at Cosford, as this was a training camp and subject to strong discipline. When my time at Cosford came to an end we had the usual drinking session, during which my new friends said they were very sorry to see me go. I was posted to RAF Wythall, near Birmingham, for a six-week course to become a fully-fledged Clerk/GD. The course was very concentrated, and I didn't think there was so much to learn about the running of the RAF. I found that I had to put every possible effort into passing the course, which I did with flying colours, thanks to a great deal of revision. Next day I found that I had been posted to RAF Burtonwood for overseas service, and then went home on fourteen days' embarkation leave.

At Burtonwood in December 1947, it was very cold. We had to assemble in a large hangar, some 500 of us, to await news of our eventual postings, and in my case this took a long time. It seems that either there were plenty of Clerks/GD overseas or few ships to carry new ones in, as I was sent home for Christmas. It was a further two weeks after the New Year that my name was finally called out, and a batch of us paraded on the square, ready to proceed to Liverpool and a troopship.

We boarded the *SS Samaria,* which was to be our temporary home, and after calling at Malta arrived at Port Said, from where we took a train to our destination, RAF El Hamra, a tented transit camp. Next morning we went to the cookhouse for breakfast, to be served by German prisoners of war who had been in the Canal Zone for five years! We were given inoculations and told to wait around until our final postings were announced. Mine turned out to be - RAF El Hamra! I was allocated to Movements section, which was short of clerks. The work was hard, but I soon became accustomed to it, and as we finished at 13.00 we had plenty of time off to explore the area. The living conditions of people in a nearby village were, we thought, awful. Flies crawled all over them, and over food they offered for sale.

At this point I must mention the treatment of Jewish airmen arriving in Egypt from the UK. Because of the sensitive position in the Middle East at that time, they were told, on arrival at El Hamra, to step forward. They were given postings in the Canal Zone, as we could not send them to RAF Stations in Palestine. Despite this, I made out the usual paperwork one day for about fifty airmen posted to Palestine. Later that day their train was blown up by Jews, and eight of our airmen were killed and a number wounded. The only people to know that they were on the train were myself, the Sergeant in charge of transport at 51 MT and of course the airmen themselves. I can only assume that the Jews had people on the station at Kantara, where the lads boarded the train. The Jews were of course very bitter with the British, who were sending back refugees to Europe as there were too many in Palestine, and the Arabs were objecting strongly, so once again Britain was 'pig-in-the-middle'. This situation became worse and worse.

All this time, it was so hot that in our off-duty hours all we wanted to do was to laze about, and we couldn't afford much else anyway. Drafts of airmen were coming in from the UK and men returning, which kept us busy at work. Due to worsening developments in Palestine, we were confined to camp for one 24-hour period, and guards were introduced every night, some of whom had to be permanent staff. At last I and a friend managed to get a 48-hour pass and go to Port Said, a very smelly place, where we stayed at the Welcome, a regular service hotel. While there, stones were thrown at us when my friend upset a local, so then we sought the sanctuary of the NAAFI.

In July the German prisoners were repatriated at long last, and their work was taken over by natives. Soon, diseases spread over the camp, particularly 'Gippy Tummy', a mild form of dysentery. I was unlucky enough to contract it, and lost over a stone in weight before I recovered.

Two WAAFs were posted in from Aden in August 1948, and one came to work in Movements section. She soon found herself a male friend and the two were always to be seen together. After six months the airman went home, but the WAAF was in the depths of despair for a very long time, as she never heard a word from her departed friend. We thought the WAAFs, who had to be specially guarded at night, were very drab and ordinary in their uniform. On the other hand, a real thrill for us came when Ivy Benson's Band toured the Canal Zone. What a grand performance that was - we clapped and cheered time and again! They really looked beautiful.

Far away, the clouds of war were gathering again

over Berlin. There was now a shortage of trained men in the RAF to cope with the extra work caused by the Berlin airlift, and a movements clerk was a valuable thing to have around. The outcome was that as we were in for the Duration of The Present Emergency we could be kept in for a longer period, in our case another three months. This was an awful blow — I sat on my bed in the depths of despair. From that day I began to drink far more than I had before. The pattern of life was — sleep, swim, guard, work, drink, smoke, and wish our time away. The guard duties became more and more of a bind, but more necessary as the situation between the Egyptians and us worsened. If a native was caught inside the camp you could shoot him provided he did not stand still on your challenge. A Corporal did shoot one, and was reduced to the ranks.

I managed to be included in a visit to Cairo organised by the YMCA. We had to wear civilian clothes and travel in a civilian bus. On arrival, we had a grand meal in a smart hotel and then visited the museum to see the mummies etc. Then we boarded the bus to be taken to the pyramids and the sphinx. I was pleased that I had made the effort.

At Christmas we had a grand dinner, served by the officers as was the tradition. There was more than any of us could eat or drink. Afterwards, some games were arranged. We went to bed that night saying that it was not too bad in the RAF, even if we were stationed at El Hamra!

As the situation in Egypt deteriorated, so the defence training increased. We had rifle and Sten practice in the trenches, which I enjoyed. Nobody was allowed out of camp unarmed, and WAAFs had to be escorted. On one occasion I had to go to Deversoir to fetch a replacement typewriter, acting as escort to a WAAF, and while there I met several of the lads that I had come out with who had been posted to Deversoir.

I started the New Year with mixed feelings. I enjoyed the work but longed for home, knowing that I had another summer to go through, whereas before Christmas I thought I would be out by May 1949 and certainly away from Egypt by early April. Guard duties became more and more of a bind, the cold wind off the desert seeming to sweep straight through me. There were also some sandstorms, which in the cold of a grey winter day were awful. When we tried to eat in the cookhouse or tent everything was covered in sand. January and February 1949 were very drab, enlivened only by my 21st birthday, spent in the tent over bottles of beer, with a trip to the NAAFI later for more beer! We managed to keep interested in a number of things through March and April, and then the weather turned warm enough for swimming. I played as much cricket as I could. Toward the middle of May, my friend Bill became due for release. I was sorry to see him go as we had been through a lot together, but realised that when he had gone I wouldn't be far behind.

In the section things became a little tiresome. The new WAAFs were making no end of mistakes, and a new chap we had was just as bad. The Berlin airlift was going well, so I hoped I would not be needed much longer. At this time we were invited to join the Royal Australian Air Force, but we would not have been allowed to go home first, which is what everyone wanted to do. I think that later in life a large number of the lads would have wished they had taken up the offer!

All the time I was in the RAF I was, together with everyone else, short of money. I was paid 35/- (£1.75) per fortnight and that didn't last more than three or four days. Towards the end we did get fifty free cigarettes each week from the RAF, and this helped. Being in the Post Office, I did get my money made up; some I gave to my mother and some, about £200 in all, I saved.

As I hoped to be on my way soon, I put in for three days' leave to allow me to go to Port Said to buy a few things for the folks at home. This time I went alone as Bill had gone home and my mate Ted was in Cyprus. Port Said had not changed — it was still smelly and dirty, and young boys still pestered you to see their sisters. But it wasn't the same; gone was the excitement that was there when Bill and I first went. Now the natives were hostile, and I had to keep to the main streets or risk being attacked. Nevertheless, I had a good time, and on the Tuesday I said farewell to the Welcome Hotel for the last time and plodded back to El Hamra.

At camp, security was becoming even tighter. Exercises were held more frequently and the guards increased. On Friday 1 July 1949 I started to 'clear' from the Station. One of my first calls was to SSQ, where the old Flt. Sgt. who I had first met at Cosford and who had looked after me when I had dysentery was sorry to hear that I was leaving. When I saw the Station Commander he shook my hand and asked me if I had put in a bad word for him, as he had once caught me with dirty boots on parade. I of course told him that I had handed over to a good man and that I was sure he would be dealt with as were all the others! He thanked me for the work I had done on the Station and said I would be missed. Whether this was true or not, I thought that those words were enough to make up for all the hard work over the eighteen months I had been in Movements.

On Monday 11 July, having said goodbye to all my friends and donated my stock of books to them, I boarded a truck to Port Said as a member of the advance party, the rest of the homeward-bound airmen travelling by train. Tuesday was spent on board the *SS Empress of Australia* watching army and RAF men coming aboard, and at 17.00 we were under way. The sea was smooth, and at first we enjoyed the trip, but soon we became bored, just wanting to get home, so the sea travel was a pain. More army and RAF personnel came aboard at Malta, and then on Friday 22 July I was looking towards land and saw what turned out to be Wales. What a lovely sight after all that sand! Next day saw us coming up the Mersey to the docks, and we, the advance party, were soon allowed on the quayside. We disembarked at 09.00 on the Sunday and caught a train to RAF Weeton, where next day all the paperwork began, but it was not until the following week that we could finally go home.

❏ Mr. Ian R. Mein (2354800)

I joined the RAF at Padgate on 14 June 1947, and after a week to be initiated moved to RAF Bridgnorth, Shropshire, for six weeks' square-bashing as a member of 11 Flight, 2 Wing. This proved for many to be quite a task; some seemed to have two left feet! One met chaps from all walks of life adjusting to the new environment. In my billet was a Sainsbury of the grocery chain, Tony Hawes, a cartoonist on the *Daily Mail* and later with the BBC, and a diamond merchant. I wonder where they are now?

After the six weeks training I was posted to RAF Netheravon in Wiltshire as a u/t fabric worker, which didn't mean anything to me at the time. On arriving at Netheravon I found it to be a base occupied by the Airborne services and for the next few weeks I was trained on glider repair work.

I had not been there long when a combined exercise, Operation 'Longstop', took place. We were all allocated special duties during the exercise, and myself and another airman were detailed to be in the VIP marquee as orderlies and temporary batmen. One job I had was opening car doors, and imagine my surprise when out of one car stepped Field Marshal Viscount Montgomery, whose first words were "This reminds me of Ascot"!

During my service, weekend leave was restricted to a 48-hour pass on alternate weekends, so to make the most of my time I used to catch the midnight train from Waterloo to Salisbury to return to camp on Sunday nights, pay a shilling (5p) for a bed at the Red Shield Club on Salisbury Station and catch the first bus to Netheravon on the Monday morning. I spent the rest of my service there, and can recall that the Station Commander was Gp. Capt. H. M. Day of Colditz fame.

It is true that you never forget your service number. After 47 years I'm still using every day the black standard-issue shoe-brush stamped with my number!

"...I was trained on glider repair work."

❏ Mr. R. Molloy (2357636)

I was called up for National Service in June 1947 and went to RAF Padgate to be kitted out, spending two weeks there. Then I was sent to RAF West Kirby for eight weeks' square-bashing and trade selection. While there I spent six days in sick quarters with tonsilitis, so missed using the Sten gun.

Then I was posted to RAF Driffield in Yorkshire, a Station which had Wellington bombers, and managed to get a flight in one before going to RAF Cosford for trade training as a flight mechanic/engines. After successfully passing out there I went to RAF Feltwell in Norfolk [3 FTS] to work on Harvards and Tiger Moths. Several incidents that happened while I was there come to mind. During the week before Battle of Britain Day several aircraft crashed. One Harvard pilot was killed when he carried out aerobatics too close to the ground, a Tiger Moth went over on its nose, and the undercarriage of a brand new Spitfire F.19 collapsed on landing. We went out to the runway to bring the Spitfire in and I was under the port wing fixing the lifting strap when the tail wheel folded up. I thought the whole lot was coming down on me! On another occasion a Wellington came in for an overnight stop and we went out in the morning to run the engines up, but as the trolley-acc. was plugged in all the bombs [presumably practice bombs - Ed.] and racks dropped out, someone having gone in during the night and switched the appropriate switches on.

When the Berlin airlift began I was posted to RAF Hullavington, then the Empire Flying School, which used Lancasters, Meteors, Buckmasters, Harvards, Ansons and Oxfords. During this time three months were added to our service but then flight mechanics were made redundant, so I only served just under two years. I managed to make flights in several of the aircraft.

At the end of my time I went to St. Anne's, near Blackpool, for demobilisation. I should have been there only one night but as the airman who should have brought our papers forgot them the process took nearly a week.

❏ Mr. D. Palmer (3105155)

Since joining the ATC in 1944, I had been interested in the RAF. I attended a medical in a very cold building in Brighton in December 1946 but was not called up until June 1947, due to an exceptionally bad winter, when many camps were closed down for lack of fuel. Firstly I was sent to RAF Padgate for

"3105155 AC2 Palmer, D..."

kitting-out and there I became AC2 Palmer D. After ten days at Padgate I was posted to RAF West Kirby for eight weeks' general service training. While the majority of the chaps there were complete strangers to one another, it so happened that there were eight others on the camp from my home town and all known to me. Bob Holness of radio and TV fame also served at West Kirby at precisely the same time, and we have since corresponded.

Following my GST course I was sent to RAF Credenhill, near Hereford, on an equipment course. Half-way through the course, the RAF decided that there were enough people in equipment and I was posted to Pool Flight. After eight weeks at Credenhill I was sent to RAF Benson as a messing orderly. Shortly after arriving there, I was put on a draft for Singapore, but after having all the inoculations and enjoying fourteen days embarkation leave, the draft was cancelled! Towards September that year, 1948, I was selected to take part in the Battle of Britain parade in London, and this was preceeded by a refresher drill course at RAF Halton, where I recall being driven mad early each morning by the apprentices blowing (I won't say playing) bagpipes.

☐ Mr. Michael Reynolds (2372308)

I did my service in the late 'forties, when all the services were in transition, with home-coming veterans anxious to return to civilian life and newcomers very much sprogs! Despite the strange feeling of having arrived at a party which finished two days ago — or was it due to start in two days' time? — I really enjoyed every minute of my time. Apart from what I regarded as an honour to serve, I was also assailed by a feeling of emancipation, of slipping away from the restraints of my parents, who incidentally were loving, caring people. I never really returned to my parental home once I was 'demobbed', and I look back with some pride and gratitude for the opportunity to have been a 'Brylcreem' Boy.

When I registered for National Service I didn't wait to be asked which service I wanted to join! Having lived, breathed and dreamed of joining the RAF, I told the chap behind the counter "I want to join the RAF". (I was a cocky lad in those days, and my wife says that nothing much has changed!). I was then enlisted into the RAF Volunteer Reserve, the normal procedure at that time [but probably not in later years — Ed.]

My service began on 14 October 1947 at RAF Padgate, a place that only an uncontrollable optimist would have found inviting. There I was sworn in, sworn at, X-rayed, kitted out, bemused and attended my first Church parade. I can't tell you how thrilled I was to march behind the Station band to the Royal Air Force March Past.

As the transformation from Mr. Michael John Renolds to AC2 Reynolds M.J. took place, I was posted to RAF Cardington, which at that time was the recruit training centre for those young men who had signed on for a regular engagement, and thus I and my colleagues were something of a novelty to the permanent staff and a curiosity to the u/t regulars. We felt incumbent to be different and somehow thought it odd that anyone would wish to make a career of the RAF — such is the ignorance of the young. We were determined to do anything they could do, but better, although I'm sure this was not put to any test.

In one respect we were 'different' in that some of us wore the dreaded beret, which was not unlike a cowpat, but despite this we all tried to carry ourselves in a 'smart and airman-like manner', and the RAF looked for nothing more than that. I must say we did a great deal of moaning about the 'bullshit' and we were not a little truculent. In the years to follow I think we would have recognised our behaviour as being rather childish. We made it clear to anyone in charge of us that we "didn't want to be in the RAF" and complained about nearly everything! These outbursts came to the notice of one of our Flight Sergeants, a former flight engineer, then serving in the RAF Regiment, and he pulled off one of the best pieces of propaganda I have witnessed before or since. He visited each of five huts of 'sprogs', asked us to stop whatever we were doing and told us to gather round. Then he said "What is all this binding about?" and went on to say that he thought we had all come from good homes where things were kept neat and tidy and clean and that we probably liked to look smart. Grudgingly we agreed. "Well, that's all we want" he said and then advised us that we had enlisted in the RAF Voluntary Reserve. A bolt of lightning couldn't have made a bigger impact. He changed us in five minutes to eager, able, very smart, proficient and dare I say it, proud airmen! We polished our billets, blancoed our webbing and attended to our brasses as if we were crown jewellers. The creases in our uniforms were dangerous, so sharp and crisp were they, and we eventually 'passed out' feeling we had achieved something special and that we ourselves had become something worthwhile.

After 'square-bashing' at RAF Cardington, my first posting was to that stronghold of the Royal

Navy, Plymouth, to RAF Mountbatten, where I quickly learned all about minority groups, long before they had been identified. The city was swamped with Royal Navy types, WRNS, Royal Marines, a battalion of the King's Own Scottish Borderers and perhaps 200 all ranks of the RAF. I quickly recalled the Flight Sergeant at Cardington and like my colleagues did not let the Junior Service down.

More than forty years on, I look back on the Service with pleasure, gratitude and pride, and when I adorn my RAFVR tie I walk a little straighter and taller. I do know that some lads hated National Service, and I'm sad for them.

❑ Mr. Peter George (3112704)

After enlisting at RAF Padgate, I was posted to RAF West Kirby for initial training and while there I obtained a 'Best Recruit' certificate, a 'Marksman' certificate and a boxing champion award. The boxing PTI instructor there was Sgt. Harry Mason, who was British light and welter weight champion about 1923. I was posted to RAF Staverton, near Cheltenham, for RAF Police training, and moved to RAF Pucklechurch, near Bristol, with that unit. The RAF Police School then made a further move, to RAF Pershore, where I served on Station duties and then as an instructor on the Police School intake section. Sgt. Mason was also posted to Pershore about the same time. Being a keen footballer, (I was on West Bromwich's books), I played at Pershore with Jimmy Wardhaugh (Hearts and Scotland), John Pickup (Stoke City) and Jeff Taylor (Fulham and Brentford).

Then I was posted to RAF Buckeburg in Germany on Provost duties, attached to 107 Flight. I performed street patrols, carying a .45 revolver and five rounds, drawn from the guardroom before every shift, and also vice patrols at Minden. I still played football, this time with Ralph Hyder (Fulham) and Peter Blakey (Blackpool), who later became the physiotherapist for Burnley.

At the end of my service I flew home in a Dakota and was 'demobbed' at RAF Hednesford.

❑ Mr. Brian Ogden (2395751)

After enlisting at RAF Padgate on 5 July 1948, I was posted to RAF Bridgnorth on 13 July for basic training. As I was a trumpeter, I was roped in for the Station band, and because of this I got out of quite a bit of training, and consequently wasn't very popular with the square-bashing NCOs.

On 15 September 1948 I was posted to the air radar school at RAF Yatesbury. Some time in mid-November I passed out as an air radar mechanic and was posted to 230 OCU, Bomber Command, at RAF Lindholme, Lincolnshire. After two or three months the unit moved to RAF Scampton, where there were eight or nine other musicians, so we formed a small band. We played at dances and parties in the officers' and Sergeants' messes and I did a lot of disc-jockeying in the airmen's mess.

One evening we were rehearsing in the band hut, where incidentally there was a full set of military band instruments, when the Station Commander sent the orderly officer to tell us that the Station was to have an AOC's inspection in about three weeks and a military band on parade on the day was required. So after three weeks of cajoling and getting NCOs to intimidate people we were ready. On the day we turned out with a 25-piece military band; the trouble was that only eight of us were playing and the rest were 'passengers'! The AOC was very impressed and as well as inspecting the guard of honour he inspected and spoke to us. Fortunately nobody slipped up. When it was all over the Station Commander was highly delighted and rewarded us with a resounding "Well done, chaps". The drummer in the band was an armourer, Eddie Taylor, who turned professional when he was demobbed and rose to play in Johnnie Dankworth's band.

I stayed at Scampton until being demobbed on 12 April 1950.

❑ Mr. E. Cobbold (2420452)

I was called up to report to RAF Padgate on 20 January 1949, and was one of about 120 recruits in a Flight. I then square-bashed for eight weeks at RAF West Kirby, where I remember doing cross-country runs in singlet, shorts and ammunition boots in the Wirral snows! We really did bash the square, too, since we were 'volunteered' to do a guard of honour for Marshal of the RAF Lord Tedder at some function in Liverpool about the end of February. It rained all day and our beautifully whitened webbing 'bled' all over our nice new greatcoats, which had to be dry-cleaned at vast expense.

Then I was sent to train as an air wireless mechanic at 2 Radio School, RAF Yatesbury, from about April to September 1949. Our lot, being 'in' for only eighteen months, were only supposed to have about three weeks training as assistants, which would just about qualify one to carry the toolkit, but I flannelled my way into the mechanics' course on the strength of knowing the difference between a valve and a light bulb!

20

On completion of the course, I filled in a form stating that I was willing to be posted overseas, but was sent to 66 Squadron, Fighter Command, at RAF Duxford, Cambridgeshire. Almost before I had a chance to unpack, the squadron moved to RAF Linton-on-Ouse in Yorkshire [7 October 1949 — Ed.]. Linton was at that time in the East Riding, so having been born in the West Riding I guess that was as close to an overseas posting I was going to get!

The squadron flew Meteor F.4s at that time and I was responsible for the aircraft R/T set; another airman looked after the IFFs. We shared a hangar with 92 Squadron and there were two Hornet squadrons as well. I spent all the rest of my time at Linton until returning to Duxford for my last week to 'clear' and was discharged on 19 August 1950. I was lucky to be released on the normal date, since the Korean unpleasantness was just getting going and our service period was to be extended by six months. However, I had been accepted for a place at teachers' training college and so slipped under the net; or perhaps they were glad to be rid of me! All in all, I enjoyed my service; it untied my mother's apron-strings and gave me self-confidence.

☐ Mr. Peter Hocking (2426067)

I joined the RAF on 10 March 1949 at Padgate and a week later was posted to West Kirby for recruit training. There our weapons-training instructors were Corporals in the RAF Regiment. We were warned about one, Cpl. Collier, whose gimmick was that he was renowned for swearing, but if any of the recruits disliked his bad language he would refrain from using it. We decided to call his bluff and one brave AC2 said that he objected to the use of bad language in any form. Collier said that he would take note of this and remember our Flight (14Q). Much to everyone's surprise, he did not swear once in front of our Flight for the rest of our training, and to this day I have always had the highest regard for the RAF Regiment — which was perhaps what Cpl. Collier intended!

On 21 April I was interviewed for a National Service commission but applied for a five-year Short Service commission in aircrew. I passed out from recruit training on 18 May 1949, at which time Flight 14Q won the 'Aspedistra' Trophy for best all-round Flight. As my posting had not come through, I remained at West Kirby until 10 June, when I was posted to Yatesbury for a radar operator's course. However, the course was 'over-booked', so I was put on fatigues until on 7 July I went to RAF Hornchurch to attend an Aircrew Selection Board. This I passed, and was selected as a navigator, but as the five-year commissions were no longer available I returned to Yatesbury to take up the radar operator course on 21 July. I passed the course, and on 13 September I had an interview with the Wing Adjutant, Flt. Lt. Clark, about the prospects of becoming aircrew. He advised me, in view of the state of the RAF at that time, to complete my

'You'll be sorreee!'

21

National Service and go back to college.

My first posting after my course was to RAF Sopley, Hampshire, a GCI station, as an AC2 radar operator Group C under training. I remember a night interception exercise which took place while I was there which involved a stream of Lancasters flying up the Channel and then turning inland to be intercepted by Mosquitos. The technique was rather like the German 'Wild Boar' system, and we broadcast the positions of aircraft leading the stream and let the Mosquitos help themselves using their AI equipment. At the end of the exercise we were told that contact had been lost with one Lancaster and one Mosquito and the Station was asked to keep a skeleton watch on the radars, while the remainder of the watch could go off duty. An hour or two later the CO came round and was surprised to see that the complete watch was still there. When he asked the radar Sergeant what was going on he was told that the whole watch had volunteered to stay. I don't know what we had hoped to achieve, but the feeling was that perhaps we might see one or both aircraft at some time. Apart from the NCOs, all the operators were National Servicemen. Unfortunately we did not see anything, and next day we heard that the dinghy from the Lancaster and part of the Mosquito were found floating in the Channel, and the theory was that they had collided. We lost nine aircrew that night, and for the next few days the atmosphere was rather subdued and morose, and while the accident was nothing to do with us we felt that it was two of 'our' aircraft which had been lost.

On 8 November 1949 I found that my aircrew application had not been cancelled as requested, and I was posted to the Aircrew Transit Unit at RAF Digby, Lincolnshire. No sooner had I arrived than the camp was put into quarantine due to a polio outbreak. I stayed there until 28 November, when I was posted yet again, this time to RAF Welford, in Berkshire. I was then given a choice of posting to any Station in Southern Signals Area, and chose RAF Gibbet Hill, a GEE station at Hindhead in Surrey, and arrived there on 1 December. It was a very small Station, and when everyone was there, which was not very often, we numbered about 80. The only officers were a Flt. Lt. as CO and a Flg. Off. as Adjutant, and there were two Sergeants. Being a GEE station it was operational 24 hours a day every day, but as we worked watches we had plenty of free time. I lived at Portsmouth at the time, so could go home quite often.

I was detached to RAF Worth Matravers, Dorset, on 4 January 1950 for a GEE course, which I passed, and returned to Gibbet Hill on 22 January. After a further period of routine work I sat and passed the AC1 examinition on 16 March. My first flight, in an Anson from RAF Hendon, was on 4 July 1950, and was in order to learn how to use airborne GEE equipment.

Although the billets were only Nissen huts the food was good (usually!), and we generally enjoyed our time at Gibbet Hill. GEE was much easier to operate than GCI, with usually not a lot happening, but when anything did go wrong with the gear we had only two minutes to get back on the air with the correct phasing, so we did have some moments of excitement! National Servicemen made up by far the greater proportion of the staff at Gibbet Hill. We decided we would be good tradesmen but not so good as airmen, and amused ourselves by 'bucking the system' when we could, but never at the expense of the Station's operational record.

My period of service was now complete, and I left Gibbet Hill on 6 September 1950 for RAF Welford, where I was demobbed three days later. Compared with others, my service was probably rather dull, but I enjoyed it.

☐ Mr. David L. Gatzias (2433212)

First, of course, came registration, and on the way I walked around the block several times before making up my mind what I was going to say. "I want to register" was out — I did not want to register! "I am required to register" sounded a little pompous, so after a few more discarded openers I settled on "I have come to register". In the Labour Exchange the manager was behind the counter, quite alone, and the place was empty. "Hello, come to register?" he said, and all I ever did say was "Yes".

Call-up was on 25 May 1949, and I travelled from Dartmouth, Devon, my home town, with another boy from a village, and we soon picked up more conscripts on the long journey to RAF Padgate. My travelling companion and I were soon parted, and we began the very strange life of square-bashing; being shouted and screamed at became quite normal. What was not normal were the attentions of the Sergeant in charge, who selected some of us for rather more intimate attention. Although just up, we knew what his intentions were and tried to avoid being called alone into his room. Later on I met a chap who told me that he had foisted his attentions on a couple of recruits who had reported him to the padre and that was the end of the Sergeant's career. I managed to get through the weeks without much incident, although I never overcame my fear of the Sten gun (it cost 2/9 to manufacture — 14p — and might blow up in your hands) and was able to pass muster on the range

"to receive one sausage..."

because some kind soul had advised me to take a round pencil with me when picking up the target for inspection and to quickly punch some holes in it whilst 'on the trot' which would pass for bullet holes!

I was then posted to RAF Credenhill, near Hereford, for trade training. As I had already studied shorthand and typing and had some Pitman's certificates to prove my proficiency, I was soon called for interviews and tests to see whether I was suitable to serve as a personal assistant to an Air Vice Marshal. There must have been an AC Schofield also selected for the privilege, for when I was called out from the classroom for yet another interview I was called Schofield. I protested as best I could, and even the class instructor attempted to tell the Sergeant it was not my name, but to no avail. I didn't get the job (did I want it?) but will never know if I was unsuitable or if it was Schofield.

At Credenhill the food was dreadful, and there was very little of it. We queued up for our main meal to receive one sausage and nothing else. Our class was the last to get to the mess hall and by this time all the bread, served from a tea-chest on the floor, had

gone, grabbed by the first-comers to fill up, and who can blame them? We were hungry, and had to go to the NAAFI to fill up. I later learned, when I was working at Air Ministry as a civilian, that there had been a scandal: the Flt. Lt. catering officer, a Sergeant in stores and the supplier of the food were in cahoots in a swindle. Even later, I worked with a man who, while on audit duty with the Air Ministry, had done the audit which had revealed the discrepancies.

After a couple of weeks at Credenhill I developed excruciating pains in my head, with pains in my body and uncontrollable shaking. I visited the MO, but did not see him, only a Sergeant who threw a couple of tablets at me and told me to go away. The next day was worse: I could hardly walk. A fellow in my hut (I still remember his name and have a photo of him) was concerned and helped me to the MI Room. I was greeted with derision by the same Sergeant. I would not go away and demanded to see the MO. After I'd thrown up on the floor I was given some attention and my temperature was taken. Before I knew it I was in an ambulance, half-conscious. Every time I woke there was the same padre with me, and he was saying prayers over me. My problem was knowing whether to say "Thankyou" or "Amen"! I said nothing, just drifted off to sleep, and when I woke I was being taken from the ambulance into a hospital which turned out to be at RAF Cosford. I was put into a room of my own and was aware that a nursing sister was looking through a connecting window at frequent intervals. To bring down my temperature two WAAF nurses bathed me all night and in the morning a familiar car drew up outside and my parents came to see me, wearing masks. My mother asked me whether I knew what was the matter with me, and as I hadn't been told she told me that I had polio. The Sister was upset and told my mother that they had been told not to tell me. I had escaped serious paralysis, and slight paralysis to the side of my face gradually disappeared. I stayed at Cosford for six weeks, then after some convalescent leave went back to Credenhill to finish my course.

After that I was posted to RAF Middle Wallop in Hampshire, where I was PA to the Station Commander — my certificates came in useful after all. This was an interesting job, in which I stayed until I was demobbed in 1951.

As I said, I did not want to register, but with the passage of time I realise that National Service did me good, and I have no regrets. I only wish that I'd known more then and could have taken advantage, but we were young and green.

❑ Mr. Frank R. Davies (2435609)

After the initial week at 1 Reception Unit at RAF Padgate, I did 'square-bashing' at RAF Bridgnorth and trade training at RAF Credenhill, Hereford. I then returned to Padgate on the permanent staff, and spent the remaining 20 months of my service there.

Reading 'Air Mail' magazine over many years, I've been surprised by the non-existence of any mention of RAF Padgate, which was the introduction to the RAF for thousands and thousands of young men. It was to all intents and purposes two units — 1 Reception Unit (1 RU) and 3 School of Recruit Training (3 SoRT), each of which had its own administration. I worked in the Central Drafting Office, which was situated within the SHQ complex far away from either the RU or the SoRT. The CDO consisted of four sections: RU Movements, handling block movements from the RU to various SoRTs; 3 SoRT Movements, concerned with individuals' movements after completion of eight weeks' recruit training; the section in which PORs and SROs were compiled; and finally Documents Section, on which I served from October 1949 to June 1951 and was i/c from June 1950, which handled documentation of recruits posted from the RU to 3 SoRT. We did not compile them — they were delivered to us each week complete, and I assumed that they were compiled at RAF Records at Gloucester or Ruislip. Certainly when we changed over from the loose sheets kept in large brown envelopes to a Cardex system we had numerous visits by officers from Ruislip. Apart from adding the green and red identity discs to each set of documents we did nothing with them until the recruit completed his training, whereupon we sent them to the respective trade training school.

My recollections of the first seven or eight days in the RU are probably the same as others have — being marched around from here to there and anywhere else by those Corporals who we thought were at least Group Captains. On returning on the permanent staff I found that they were mainly orderlies with five or six years' service who had signed on the 'Bounty Scheme', serving four years and being paid for five. I think they had mostly gone by the end of 1950.

Duty clerk was a duty we all did every couple of months or so, and quite often we would receive a 'phone call from Mother asking to speak to her son who had joined a couple of days previously. We would tell them to call back in thirty minutes and then Tannoy for the recruit in question to report to the Duty Clerk's room in SHQ. Not knowing what was afoot, terrified lads knocked on the door and usually became very embarassed when we told them why they were there. In addition, many parents and girl friends would turn up at the main gate on Sundays asking to see the new recruits and we would duly oblige. The human side of RAF Padgate!

While on duty we were allowed to use the RU's NAAFI. Obviously a well-worn uniform stood out from all the brand new ones and usually brought a question and answer session. I think one of the worst aspects of those first few days was a complete lack of information on what was to happen next. The funny side was hearing recruits with six days' service telling others with three days' service to "Get some in" or "Get your number dry".

We also shared a security patrol with the recruits in four or five hour shifts through the night. These were introduced following thefts and attempted thefts from the massive clothing store. The recruits had a baton and we took a torch. I'm glad to say I never saw anything.

Padgate was not an easy camp for the staff. Discipline was strict, and I recall the SWO telling us that we were the first RAF personnel the recruits would see and therefore we had to set an example at all times. We had a working parade every morning except Wednesday, when there was a CO's parade. There were regular kit inspections and at all times we had our webbing on display, and all that implies. All the National Service Corporals were demobbed during April and May 1950 and the LACs who took their place as Section i/cs remained LACs. We were regularly assured by our Warrant Officer and others that the situation would be resolved — it never was! Had we signed on for another year we would have been regulars. We did have one three-year man, who was the only Corporal in the whole SHQ at one time. I'm sure this attitude was not confined to Padgate.

❑ Mr. Keith Hyatt (2478427)

About 27 June 1950, at the age of eighteen years and three months, I travelled with many others to RAF Padgate, to be met at Warrington station in the pouring rain by a number of lorries. I spent a week at Padgate, during which time we were kitted out with most of our clothing and a number of deficiency chits, which in my case were for a large pack and one or two minor items. I never did receive a large pack! We soon got into the swing of things, with a short-back-and-sides, visits to the camp tailor to have trouser legs adjusted, and one or two lectures. As I had School Certificate I was classed as POM (Potential Officer Material). The day after I arrived

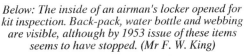

Below: The inside of an airman's locker opened for kit inspection. Back-pack, water bottle and webbing are visible, although by 1953 issue of these items seems to have stopped. (Mr F. W. King)

Above: An airman's typical bed layout for inspection. From the foot of the bed are the boots and shoes, each with a spare pair of laces; mug; on the towel are two mess tins; brushes for shoes and clothes; soap; 'irons'; razor; comb; shaving brush; toothbrush; button stick; boot polish; above the towel are socks, collars and gloves; then come shirts, pullovers, kitbag and tie; and finally blankets; great coat, tunic and peaked cap (often irreverently referred to as a 'brothel-bonnet'. Where are you now Airman 2562105? (Mr F. W. King)

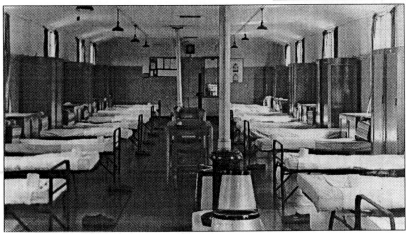

Inside a typical barrack hut at RAF Hednesford. Floors are highly 'bulled', stoves blackened and surrounds whitened, towels draped over 'pits' with mugs on top, sheets and blankets neatly boxed, shoes under the foot of each bed. Note that the beds here were arranged 'top to toe'. At the end of the room, next to the mirror, is a poster showing the standard kit layout and above the door is the Tannoy loudspeaker. (Mr D. Turnidge.)

Above: A familiar sight at any RAF School of Recruit Training - the Main Gate. This one was at RAF Hednesford. At the picket post two SPs can be seen inspecting passes while two airmen, probably recruits, stand by the gates. The main guardroom is to the right of the picture. On the kitbag of the airman in 'civvies' can be seen his service number, which could be either 2535095 or 3135095. If newly issued, these numbers date the picture at around October 1951. (Mr D. Turnidge).

Below: A typical group of recruits at the end of their basic training; the 'inmates' of Hut 148 at RAF Hednesford in March 1952, with DIs Cpl. Wall and Sgt Tait. (Mr D. Turnidge).

at Padgate one of my colleagues from work, who was a day younger than I, arrived, and I was able to yell out "Get some service in"! We soon learned barrack-room songs, and we paid a number of visits to the camp cinema, where I recall seeing Doris Day in 'My Dream Is Yours'. Our civilian clothes were sent home in our suitcases and we were told that only after trade training would we be allowed to have 'civvies' in camp again. However, we kept our own pyjamas, as at that time they were not issued. I had never worn a loose collar and studs before. Shoes were not issued either, just hob-nailed boots for 'square-bashing' and rubber-soled boots without toe-caps for best. My battle-dress tunic had lapels, but others were the earlier style with hooks and eyes. Best-blue trousers were tapered, whereas battledress trousers were wider, for wear with gaiters.

At the end of the week at Padgate I and several others were sent to 7 SoRT, RAF Bridgnorth, where I spent eight enjoyable (!) weeks. One incident that happened there was when the Station Warrant Officer had a shouting-match with a chubby-faced young Plt. Off. for not saluting the RAF flag as he passed it! At Bridgnorth I went before a Flt. Lt. to see if I was suitable officer material, and he said that my failing was my lack of knowledge of current affairs, which didn't surprise me. In any case, the officer training course would have lasted almost until my release, even though the eighteen-month stint had, during my time at Bridgnorth, been raised to two years due to the Korean war. Every effort was made to get us to sign on for two years by tempting us with regulars' pay, though the added six months attracted the extra money. However, I already had a good civilian job, so I didn't want to sign on. Also at Bridgnorth we were allocated our future trades. Because of my interest in natural history (my hobby and my work), I applied for falconry, but there were no vacancies for National Servicemen. I am also mechanically-minded, so I suggested instrument mechanic, but again there were no vacancies. Armourer was suggested, and that sounded quite interesting, so that was it.

After home leave I journeyed to RAF Kirkham for the armament course. It was initially a 22-week course, but the RAF introduced the New Trade Structure, in which courses were approximately halved so that more time could be spent on the job and less in the classroom. As the new structure was being introduced in phases, my course was cut to sixteen weeks. Instructors were mostly civilians. At Kirkham I met one of my cycling club mates and we got permission from the Physical Fitness Officer to bring our bikes to camp so that we could go out on sports afternoons. At the end of the course we were all promoted to AC1 and were informed of our onward postings. A handful of us were sent to RAF North Coates, near Grimsby.

North Coates was the headquarters of 5131 Bomb Disposal Squadron. After only a few days there we were sent to different Bomb Disposal Flights: I went to RAF Feltwell in Norfolk, which was mainly a Flying Training School. On arrival late at night I was ushered into a two-storey barrack block built of brick and resembling my 1920s-built school in south-east London, and the resemblance was confirmed when in a bed opposite was one of my former classmates! Next day I met other members of the Flight, headed by a Warrant Officer and a Flt. Lt. Soon the Flight travelled by truck to Mudeford, between Christchurch and Bournemouth, where we were housed in a Nissen hut behind a large house occupied by the army. From there we made daily sorties to an area of the New Forest where we used mine detectors to search for unexploded bombs. We found none. One weekend while I was at home on a 36, I received a telegram ordering me to return direct to Feltwell, where several of us were told that we were going to North Coates to do a bomb disposal course. The ten-week course involved arming and disarming a Lancaster, arming and defusing empty bombs and shells, and studying the workings of a German V1. They didn't have a V2 at North Coates!

The course ended in early May 1951, when four of us were to be sent to RAF Biggin Hill, only twelve miles from my home. However, at the last moment the Biggin Hill Flight was transferred to RAF Detling, the home of RAFVR officers doing gliding, so there we went. I was put in charge of generators and pumps. Again I went cycling on sports afternoons, which usually amounted to going home after lunch (30 miles) and returning early next morning. We drew old khaki army uniforms and denims for field work, had black plastic cap badges, gum-boots and sea-boot stockings and a third pair of boots or shoes. From Detling we made short trips to other places, such as a farm near Ashford where the farmer thought he had found an unexploded bomb (he hadn't), Boscombe Down on Salisbury Plain, where we dealt with a few unexploded shells, and the REME Depot at Dorchester so that we could sweep an old range at Abbotsbury. There we were christened 'Fred Karno's Army' because of our working clothes. At Dorchester nobody wore headgear as the army didn't want everyone saluting all the time. I caused a stir in the NAAFI by buying some Brylcreem, which I'd always used anyway.

On one of the journeys back to Detling we called

at RAF Middle Wallop for petrol and a meal. When we arrived at the barrier a Corporal emerged and stared at our muddy Bedford QL for a while. Then he admonished our driver for his casual appearance and sunglasses and started asking why the vehicle had red mudguards and BD painted back and front. When the driver explained he refused to believe it and became more angry. At this point our Warrant Officer, also in sunglasses and sitting next to the driver, decided it was time to have words with the Corporal as we were all hungry. What followed is probably unprintable, but we were soon sitting down to a well-earned meal, all grinning from ear to ear! When we departed our driver gave a rendering of the RAF March Past on the QL's horn!

My last field trip from Detling was to RAF Eynsham, near Oxford, where there was a large quantity of aircraft ammunition to be disposed of. We would probably be there for ten days or so, we were told, but the weather was wet for days on end and the low cloud meant that we could not cause explosions. I think we spent some six or eight weeks there before we returned to Detling.

During the stay at Detling our CO (the Flt. Lt.) asked if any of us wanted to go to North Coates to be tested for promotion to LAC. We all said we preferred to stay at Detling. Shortly afterwards we learnt that we had all been made LAC anyway and were supplied with arm badges.

At the end of June 1952 I travelled to North Coates for 'demob'. Happy days!

☐ Mr. Ken Elsley (2480080)

I was called for my medical at Bethesda Schools, Hanley, Stoke-on-Trent, on 22 June 1950, just about the time the Korean War broke out. This caused my mother some concern. She said "Do you think they'll send you there?". With the confidence of youth I replied "No, I'll ask them to send me somewhere hot like Egypt".

Being graded A.1, which is rather higher than I would be now, I was ordered to report to RAF Padgate on 11 July. There I not only received my kit but also my first experience of being on cookhouse fatigues. A consolation was, I remember, having several helpings of peaches and custard! A couple of days later, we were sent by train to Wolverhampton, where we boarded wagons going to RAF Bridgnorth, which was to be my home for the next couple of months or so. Surprisingly, I found I was able to adapt quite well to the square-bashing life. We had a fairly reasonable Sergeant and a couple of decent Corporal DIs, but I was not too keen on another Corporal, Cpl. Slater from South Shields. I

can remember him spitting in my eye as he stood with his face six inches from mine and said " Put a bloody blade in next time you shave". Darn it, I'd only been shaving about three weeks and wasn't used to it!

Drill I found not too bad, once I'd become hardened to the feel of the rifle hitting my shoulder when sloping arms. I did enjoy the rifle range, discovering that I was quite a good shot with the Lee-Enfield. I still have the targets with lots of holes spattered over them. However, the gunnery NCO wasn't too pleased when I went on the Sten gun. I'd been firing away merrily for some seconds when I realised that he was screeching something in my ear. I saw that I'd been tearing open the sandbags at the top of the butts. Apparently, this wasn't what I should have been firing at!

During the two or three weeks leading up to Battle of Britain Day we had been practicing hard on a PT display which we had been told would be put on before the public. We thought perhaps we would be going to Farnborough or somewhere as well known, but our destination turned out to be a little village in the wilds of Shropshire called Broseley, so we were a bit disappointed.

The threat of being re-Flighted which had been at the back of our minds through the weeks never materialised, and eventually our postings came through. I was told I was going to Kasfareet, which of course I'd never heard of. After passing out, eleven of us who had overseas postings were sent to RAF Hednesford, which was then a transit camp. Three days before we were due to leave for overseas, an NCO came into our billet and told us we would not get any embarkation leave unless we lived within thirty miles of Hednesford. Being only ten miles from home, I qualified, so was able to dash home for a quick 36-hour weekend.

On Tuesday 10 October 1950 we caught a train to London and from there took the boat train to Harwich. About midnight we boarded an old tramp steamer, the *Valetta,* which took us across to the Hook of Holland. After two days there, we caught a train which took us on what proved to be a fantastic journey through Germany and Austria and into northern Italy. It was one of the greatest experiences of my life to date, only slightly marred by the fact that there were five of us to a compartment. This meant that two could sleep on the seats, one between the seats and two on the luggage racks! We tossed up, and I slept on a luggage rack, which is not comfortable, I assure you!

About 06.00 on the Saturday morning, we boarded the *SS Oxfordshire* at Trieste. I imagine this ship was built about the same time as the

Titanic : it certainly resembled it, having four funnels. We sailed down the Adriatic, through the Ionian Sea and into the Med., then across to Tobruk, wher some hundreds of soldiers and airmen disembarked. We then travelled along to Port Said, docking early on 19 October. A train took us to 107 MU, RAF Kasfareet, on the edge of the Great Bitter Lake.

I settled in quickly at Kasfareet, but in January 1951 I was sent on detachment to RAF Abu Sueir, which was MEAF Headquarters. There were so many Air Vice Marshals, Air Commodores, etc., there that it was easier to walk round with one's right hand permanently at the salute!

I found that my job was escort duty on Bedford trucks travelling back and forth to Cairo twice a week to colect locally-made furniture for the married quarters. Talk about a cushy number! I took a Sten gun with me but had to leave it at an army checkpoint at Tel-el-Kebir, as armed troops were not allowed into the Delta. Thus began six quite pleasant months with two or three nights a week in Cairo. I took the chance to visit the Pyramids and Sphinx, and recall seeing King Farouk in a big red Rolls-Royce. He was married while I was in Cairo. I became friendly with an elderly taxi-driver who taught me to write my name in Arabic, which I can still do. One of the less pleasant things about the journey to Cairo was regularly being stoned as we passed through he village of Bilbeis. I'm sure that the local youths stacked a pile of rocks in readiness for us. We couldn't wind up the windows in case they got broken, so we just had to duck down and hope for the best.

In May 1951 I returned to Kasfareet, where I stayed until the end of that year. Trouble with the Egyptians had brewed up, and a number of servicemen had been killed by terrorists. Local labourers had been intimidated and had withdrawn their services. Among other things, this meant that there were no dockers at Port Said to unload supplies. The British answer was to send detachments of troops and airmen to do the work. I was detailed, and spent January and February 1952 working on a number of cargo ships.

About the end of February I was posted back to Kasfareet, where I stayed until due for release. I left RAF Fayid on 26 June in a Hastings aircraft, but there were still a few interesting moments to come. We landed at Malta and stayed there for two days while engine troubles were sorted out. This involved two or three test flights, and I can recall wondering whether we would crash into the Alps, but oddly this didn't seem to worry me! We finally landed at RAF Lyneham at 02.00 on Sunday 29 June. The rest of the weekend we spent at a tiny RAF Station called Clyffe Pypard; from there I went to London and caught a train to Lytham St. Anne's, where I was discharged on 2 July 1952. In truth, National Service was a part of my life I would hated to have missed. Happily, during the last three years I have managed to contact some of the lads who were with me, and now we keep in regular touch.

❏ Mr. Larry Mortimer (2489050)

I was called up in 1949, but as I was studying for School Certificate the Board deferred me until 1950. At the pre-service medical I was classed as Grade 2, I think because I did not have hairs on my chest to indicate maturity!

Like everybody taken into the RAF, when I arrived at RAF Padgate I was pleasantly surprised by the reception, which included a cup of tea and a room with arm chairs. Little did I foresee the change to be experienced at the drill camp! We were trade tested, and I was told by the Sgt. that for all my School Certificate I was not very bright — he seemed to take a delight in saying that. My pals told me to apply for flying, because holding a School Cert., which few in my intake did, was the basic requirement. I felt that flying would be dangerous and I also recalled what the Sgt. had said, so I plumped for a medic.

A week was spent at Padgate being kitted out with one battle-dress, one 'best blue' in which the battle-dress blouse was replaced by a tunic, shirts and separate collars, sky-blue socks, wollen gloves and a beret (later replaced by a peaked cap, I believe) [Not replaced, just supplemented by — Ed.]. Other items were a greatcoat, a pair of boots, a pair of walking-out shoes, PT shorts and vests, and earthenware mug, 'irons' (cutlery, on which the recruit stamped his service number, which I've never forgotten), and a small gospel containing a message from the King and words and music for two hymns. My 'best blue' tunic was not well tailored at the back, so the RAF fastened the too-wide gap with a press-stud. I didn't expect such attention to detail!

While at Padgate I saluted a Warrant Officer in mistake for a commissioned officer [That makes two of us! — Ed.] and in bringing my arm down smartly cut myself on the 'irons' I was carrying — natural justice, I suppose. We were not allowed out of camp, probably because we were such a shambles. At the end of the week, trains took us to our basic training Stations: for me, RAF Wilmslow, near Manchester.

What a transformation from Padgate! Here we

were 'broken in' to the Service. Many times after returning from drill I found my bed roll, which had to be stacked perfectly — sheet/blanket/sheet and wrapped in another blanket and squared off — knocked to the ground by the inspecting Cpl. DI. There was floor polishing and use of the 'bumper', a manual polisher which consisted of a broom-handle attached to a heavy weight which in turn was wrapped in thick cloth. This was usually placed on a thick felt pad and was drawn up and down the floor until the lino had an appearance of glass. Nobody was allowed to walk on the floor in footwear but had to step on felt pads placed at the doorways. With such discipline the billet was always spotless and the floor like a mirror. Each night there was boot cleaning, blancoing belts, gaiters and webbing and polishing buttons, with either Brasso, Silvo or Duraglit. A card with a slot could be bought to protect the uniform while cleaning buttons. From time to time there would be a full kit inspection, when the whole kit had to be laid out in a set display. Boots were dealt with either by burning the cap on the hot barrack stove, without burning the stitches, which would cause the boot to fall apart, with drastic consequences; or by spitting on the heels and toecaps and applying much polish, often with a toothbrush handle, and boning in the polish before working up to a high gloss with a rag. The DIs' heels and toecaps always looked like glass; I wonder who cleaned them. The DIs also had perfectly-hung trousers by putting small weights in the bottom of the trousers where they tucked into their gaiters.

Drill, which formed much of our eight weeks' training, was marching, entailing various movements, and saluting, without and later with arms. There was also PT. I glowed when the PTI congratulated me, a 'sprog', on a good vault over the horse. Little did he know that in civilian life I would became a PE teacher — perhaps he inspired me. There was a run and march outside the camp in our PT kit, which finished in style with the singing of 'Tzena Tzena' as we neared the back gate. We also fired .303s and Brens on the range; how different they were from our drill weapons, which were not greased. Although I enjoyed the drill, I recall being sworn at for a poor 'Present arms'; the words the DI used were "Are you trying to get a cheap thrill?" because I had poked the rifle butt into my 'privates'! Between training sessions there were NAAFI breaks — how we looked forward to them! Tea and delicious cakes; my favourites were Russian Slice and Custard Slice. And there was music from the loudspeakers — 'Bewitched', Tzena Tzena' and 'Silver Dollar'. Whenever I hear 'Bewitched' it brings back nostalgic memories, and I always ask for it at a local hotel when requests are offered.

Near the end of our training we did guard duty at the main gate, wearing all our webbing and taking all we needed for five days at the guardroom. I think we did two hours on and four hours off, and there was no guard duty at night. The two guards moved like clockwork soldiers when going the 15 paces or saluting officers of different ranks. They were difficult to identify — hand on the butt of the rifle for those below Wg. Cdr. and a full 'Present Arms' for Wg. Cdrs. and above. Recognition had to be made early so as to complete the manoeuvre by the time the officer drew level with you.

The day of our Passing-out Parade arrived. It was a ceremony not to be forgotten, with everyone immaculately turned out, bayonets gleaming and the band playing. Unfortunately it was raining, so the parade was held in a hangar and we wore greatcoats with webbing belts outside. It was not easy to hear the commands, as the hangar echoed, but we didn't falter; because of the rehearsals we knew what to expect. I almost dropped my rifle in my eagerness to 'present arms' with panache. The stock of the rifle was to be smacked hard to get the crash of the salute. (We were told to pretend to faint if we dropped our rifle and to fall with it.) Later I was singled out for a word with the Station Commander, a Gp. Capt., as he moved down the lines; he asked me what I intended to do in the RAF. Before leaving for trade training, 16 Flight, 'D' Squadron had a wonderful drunken night at the local 'Raven' pub. I recall how beautifully some of the recruits sang. 'Little White Cloud' and 'Show Me The Way To Go Home' saw us on our way back to RAF Wilmslow for the last time.

I was told to go on leave and then report to RAF Moreton-in-Marsh, Gloucestershire, the medical training school. It was a wartime Station; signs such as Aircrew Briefing Room, although painted over, could still be seen on doors, and it was said to have been the Station where Richard Murdoch was based and had the idea for his radio programme 'Much Binding in the Marsh'. We were lectured in anatomy, physiology, hygiene, first aid and nursing. The airfield was in use for flying training at the time [as the satellite of RAF Little Rissington — Ed.], and every day Harvards would take off and land, which relieved the boredom of the training as Nursing Attendant. I recall plane crashes, one of them on the WAAF bath-house, and it was said that the pilot deliberately chose that spot!

Once, on returning from leave early to laze around and get up when I felt like it I was ordered to join others in clearing snow from runways. I also saluted an inspecting officer without a cap, but on another occasion was complimented on a smart salute "for a medic", not usually the smartest of airmen. Tea at a quaint teashop in the village of Moreton-in-Marsh was a regular pleasure for me at weekends.

After the final examination, qualifying and receiving those 'dogs' (lapel badges bearing the snake and staff with crown and wings), I was posted back to Padgate. Medics were allowed a choice of area; I chose the hospital at RAF West Kirby, near Liverpool, which was my home area, but was sent to the MI room at Padgate, a stroke of luck in the end because I heard later that hospitals were hard work, and in any case Padgate was not far from Liverpool.

My duties included giving tablets (I once gave too many aspirins to a patient and was worried for some days, but he survived); giving menthol inhalers to recruits with colds; testing urine and eyesight; measuring the chests of those having medicals; and giving TABT injections. The doctors who prescribed the treatments were Flt. Lt. Burrows (who became a Sqdn. Ldr.), Shaw and Danziger. NCO in charge of the section was Flt. Sgt. Frostick, a very likeable man. Later I did clerking duty for Sqdn. Ldr. Burrows and witnessed many interesting diagnoses; one patient would not disclose his sexual escapades until I had left the room!

Ward duty at night in the hospital was one of my jobs. This involved cooking for the Corporal wardmaster (plenty of very good food — no expense too great for the National Servicemen!) and answering calls for the ambulance. Most of the calls were from barracks where the recruits were suffering from the injections, although we did once carry an attractive young female in pyjamas to the hospital. We had some fun: one cold night we told new recruits to parade naked in a billet at a certain time for an FFI (Free From Infection) examination. We did not show up, and wondered how long they stood there shivering!

Although I played football for my section, that could not prevent me being sent to RAF Lyneham for training as a Casualty Air Evacuation Attendant and subsequently flying in a Hastings to Singapore with two nursing Sisters and Australian aircrew to bring back troops wounded in Korea. After the 'bull' of Padgate it was a relief to spend days and nights at RAF Castel Benito (Libya), RAF Luqa (Malta), RAF Habbaniya (Iraq), RAF Negombo (Ceylon) and RAF Changi (Singapore) in comparative freedom with some luxury — individual chairs and no washing of 'irons' in a communal trough. The patients were stretcher cases, some of whom had injured lungs and had to receive oxygen when the plane increased altitude. Apart from patients there were soldiers, sailors and airmen returning to

Britain. We were well-equipped for our task; in additon to medical gear we had plenty of tinned food, sweets and cigarettes and a box of 'goodies' presented by the Red Cross.

On my return to Padgate I was charged with putting pleats in the back of my battle-dress, a legacy of my freedom overseas, and had to report to the guardroom each day for three days. Life in the MI room carried on without incident. When Armistice Day approached, some of the permanent staff were picked to parade in Padgate village. One chap didn't like drill so I took his place for £1. The irony is that when we were inspected before the parade I was ordered to get a new 'best blue', which cost more than the £1 I had received! We wore white webbing for the ceremony and looked very smart.

I went to RAF Lytham St. Annes for an exam for promotion to SAC. The exam was in two parts: a test of educational attainment, from which I was exempt by virtue of the School Certificate, and the oral test on nursing. At night school in Liverpool I studied German without much success, and stayed at home in nearby Wallasey on those nights, returning to Padgate in the morning. The RAF, and particularly the education officers, were keen for airmen to further their education and encouraged them in every way. Not long before demobilisation I was promoted to Acting Corporal. Now I could, as wardmaster, have my meals prepared by the nursing attendant on duty, dish out the orders and draw the gate guards to attention as I passed! My mind went back to 'square-bashing', when I would quickly come to attention when an NCO came in sight.

When the time came to leave the RAF another medical categorised me as Grade 1. The RAF had matured me. I was interviewed by an officer who tried to persuade me to stay in, and I was tempted, as I was enjoying life and was looking forward to another trip overseas. I always seemed to have money to spend, even at something like 12/- (60p.) per day. However, my aunt felt that a profession was what I needed, so I took up a post as an untrained teacher at a private school. After furthering my education over a long period, I am now a tutor at the University of Zimbabwe. Perhaps a message from this story is that if an RAF Sergeant tells you that you aren't very bright, don't be put off!

❑ Mr. E. Croson (2504823)

I was with the RAF from 30 January 1951 to 22 February 1953, and enlisted at RAF Padgate for kitting-out, medicals and inoculations. Then on to RAF Weeton, near Blackpool, for eight weeks training. The CO was Sqdn. Ldr. Darling, our drill instructor was Cpl. Jones, a real swine [not his real name! — Ed.]. 'Bull' night was on Thursdays, and CO's inspection next day. I lived in hut W39 in 8B Flight. Reveille was at 06.30, and we were on parade at 07.30 for breakfast. At 08.30 we paraded for a cross-country run in shorts and tee-shirts. The water we used for washing and shaving was cold and black, and came from an old wartime static water tank.

After training we had seven days leave and returned to camp to find that our billet had been vandalised. All the beds, bedding, lockers, fire buckets, etc., were piled up in the middle of the floor. We had to clean all this up for CO's inspection in the morning; imagine the scuffle we had to get it ready by 22.00 hours! [One wonders whether this might have been done deliberately to test the recruits' reaction — Ed.]. Soon we were posted to RAF Exminster, Devon, with temporary accommodation at Topsham barracks. Then on to RAF Exeter, where there were newly-painted billets. There was a new iron stove in the middle of the floor with an asbestos flue pipe, so we lit a fire in it, and at 20.30 the chimney exploded, scattering asbestos fragments everywhere and injuring some of the airmen. Luckily I escaped.

After a few months I was posted to RAF Bowlee, near Manchester as a cook II for three months. As I was about to return to Exeter, it was the time of the Queen's Birthday parade. As we all stood to attention for the salute the heavens opened and we all got wet through. We were then dismissed and I travelled back to Exeter, a 15-hour journey, in a wet uniform. However, I arrived and was demobilised in February 1953.

❏ Mr. Peter H. Kilmister (3131504)

We arrived at RAF Padgate on a cold, foggy evening in February 1951. As the bus passed through the main gate someone pointed to the water tower and said "Some bloke jumped off that last week"!

About four days later, after the kitting-out formalities, we were marched to the camp cinema and there, seated on the stage, were two officers. Until then, the highest rank we had met was Corporal, especially the one in the airmen's mess whose function was to spot impatient recruits banging their 'irons' together and send them to the back of the queue. (He never spotted the hungry lads who slipped slices of bread under their battledress and cheap margarine into their mugs for making toast on the coke-burning stove in the cold wooden hut!).

The job of these officers was to persuade the recruits to volunteer as aircrew. The advice "Never volunteer for anything" was still ringing in my ears, but if one possessed School Leaving Certificate and passed the medical, aircrew trainees had the advantage of not being posted to a square-bashing camp, this being replaced by 'light foot-drill', — so they said! I had never made use of my School Cert. and had no doubt about my fitness, so I found myself as part of the stampede to the front.

Soon three of us from our hut were transferred to the Aircrew Hut. We had hardly crossed the threshold before we heard for the first time and by no means the last — "Pads!". The occupant nearest the door indicated a pile of felt squares and explained that one was to be placed under each foot and a skating motion employed to perambulate about the room, thus maintaining a highly-polished floor. He added that extra spit-and-polish was necessary as AVM Garity was due to make an inspection. Next morning on the parade ground we met Mr. Garity, not an AVM but a little red-faced Corporal whose job it was to keep the Aircrew Flight occupied by marching them up and down the square morning and afternoon, in the cold, fog and rain.

The occupants of Aircrew Flight hut came under various categories; those waiting to make the journey to Aircrew Selection Board at RAF Hornchurch; those who had returned successfully and who were awaiting posting to the holding camp at RAF Driffield; the unsuccessful candidates who were on their way to ground duties training; and those who had not quite passed the medical and who would return to Hornchurch if they could overcome whatever shortcoming the medical board had identified. Thus, when not parading in the foul weather, some individuals could be found sitting on the edge of their beds trying to cross their eyes or, with nose between finger and thumb, trying to pop their ears.

One morning, Cpl. Garity included my name in his Hornchurch list, followed by his routine announcement "All them as is going to 'ornchurch in Hessex will draw their 'aversack rations". Then he made a statement which was so unusually sensible that I, for one, believed it. "The 'ornchurch people will need to be called at 05.00 hours and they will place a towel at the foot of their beds so that only the people concerned need to be woken". Next morning at 05.00 hours the door was banged open and a loud voice called "Wakey wakey, all them as is going to 'ornchurch"!

We boarded the train at Warrington bound for Euston. Very soon, something white flew past the carriage window, then another, followed by several more. Hungry airmen had opened their haversack rations and discovered the uneatable cheese sandwiches. The fellow sitting next to me was not surprised; he had worked in the cookhouse and knew that the strong-tasting margarine had been melted and applied to the thick bread slices with a shaving brush.

I was fortunate to be selected for pilot training. Many who aspired to it were disappointed when offered air gunner or signaller training, and many others were bitterly disappointed to be offered nothing at all. On the underground train taking us back to Euston I saw one 18-year-old in tears.

Four of us bypassed the intermediate camp at Driffield and were posted directly to RAF Digby in Lincolnshire to make up the numbers on a course for 'ab initio' pilot training. We arrived hours before the Driffield contingent, and after the wooden huts of Padgate and Hornchurch the modern brick-built two-storey blocks at Digby were a welcome sight. Our early arrival gave us the opportunity to select less damp blankets from the store; then we were informed that beds were allocated alphabetically, and the four of us were split up into separate rooms. Worse still, sleeping was to be head to toe, and as my bed was an even number I must sleep with my feet to the wall. (Consequently I was always the second man awake as the first man always brushed my face with his sponge-bag on his way to the washroom).

The fifteen other occupants of my room duly arrived; they had already established some camaraderie with their group but somehow I fitted in within a few days. Many of them had joined the RAF straight from school; well-known public schools like Eton, Harrow and Charterhouse were represented on the course, but a few of us had experienced life in a work place for a couple of years. I had worked for eighteen months as a temporary civil servant at an RAF Maintenance Unit where the office managers were all serving RAF officers, so I thought I had gained some insight into service life.

Next day we met the man in charge, Sqdn. Ldr. Slade, and his assistant, Flt. Lt. Webb. We were addressed as 'gentlemen', in complete contrast to the names the Corporal drill instructor had called us. Apart from explaining the shape of the course, Sqdn. Ldr. Slade lost no time in imparting a thought which he considered important to potential officers: that we should read T. E. Lawrence's "Seven Pillars of Wisdom". He went on to complain about one aspect of the system with which he indignantly disagreed: the fact that confidential reports concerning officers were open to scrutiny by ordinary airmen at RAF Records Office. Eight

weeks later I had reason to remember this.

Entering the cadets' mess for the first evening meal, we were amazed at the variety of jam, honey, marmite, and sandwich spread that the senior course members were tucking into. Reaching for a jar, we were quickly told to keep our hands off and buy our own. So mean was the catering that if, for example, the midday meal offered jam tart for sweet, there would be no jam with the evening meal.

A typical day was spent half on the airfield awaiting one's turn to do circuits and bumps in a Tiger Moth and the other half running from one classroom to another to attend three or four lectures on the dozen or so subjects covered by the course. After the evening meal we fell in on the square and marched up and down for three or four hours until the Sergeant DI was satisfied. So much for light foot drill! We learnt slow marching and rifle drill and every Saturday morning, after a rigourous room inspection, we marched around the camp before assembling as part of a large parade on the square.

The course lasted for twelve weeks. Rumour had it that at least a third of us would go no further than this 'ab initio' stage, and in the end only about 15% would get their wings. As for the failures, they would be remustered as 'bog wallahs' [Ed.] as the RAF did not take kindly to those who 'stubbed their toe on the moon'.

Six weeks elapsed and the course ahead of us passed out. The AOC, arriving by air to take the parade, was greeted by the sardonic slogan Butlins which someone had painted on the water tower. Evening 'square-bashing' intensified when we became the senior course, and much boot polish and Blanco was consumed, making inroads into our slender financial resources. Out of the National Serviceman's pay of 28/- (£1.40) per week a sum was set aside to enable successful cadets to open a bank account when they became Acting Pilot Officers. Saturday afternoons and evenings were the only opportunities we had to visit the NAAFI to spend our few shillings. Occasionally we visited Lincoln but did not stay as the best pubs were unofficially reserved for officers and out of bounds to mere cadets. The nearest pub was at Scopwick; five of us often walked there and back, my only memory being that not one of the dart-playing regulars ever spoke to us!

Once again, I disregarded advice and volunteered to help at a model aircraft flying display by erecting a marquee. With another half-dozen airmen, I waited for an hour in the cold for someting to happen. At last the hangar doors rolled open, a lorry drove in and the driver, wearing old clothes and a day's beard, alighted. He addressed me in a pseudo-Oxford accent: "Take your hands out of your pockets". When I worked at the RAF MU I had often heard civilian drivers jokingly harassing the airmen who worked in the stores, so I gave him a knowing smile and in a friendly tone replied "**** off". The driver appeared to want to continue this game as he angrily asked my name and how long I had been at Digby. I told him as I walked away — as far as I was concerned the marquee could erect itself. It was then that I realised that the airmen were standing to attention, and the driver announced that he was the second-in-command, Flt. Lt. Webb! He sent for me a few days later and said that perhaps I would be happier in another aircrew category, such as signaller or air gunner, both open to NS men and carrying the rank of Sergeant.

I was posted forthwith to RAF Innsworth, near Gloucester, to the Aircrew Allocation Unit. It was mid-morning when I entered my allocated hut, to find several airmen sprawling about and a Corporal sitting on a bed. At Padgate and Digby all Corporals were treated with great respect, so I marched smartly to him and announced myself. He and his friends fell about! My highly-polished boots and brasses caused more mirth.

My room-mates were regular airmen (some of them Halton 'brats') who had remustered for pilot training in Kenya, had failed their courses and were awaiting reselection to other aircrew categories or to ground duties. The unit was run by two middle-aged, genial if world-weary, Sergeants who demanded minimal standards of discipline. Roll calls were held twice daily, but some men arranged for friends to answer for them if they wanted to leave camp for a time. The purpose of the roll call was to allocate odd jobs in the camp, but there was always more men than jobs, so it was possible to vanish to the Salvation Army canteen or elsewhere. Amazingly, the strength of the unit trebled once a week on pay parade! Our un-airmanly conduct did not go unnoticed, and we were constantly threatened with posting across the camp to the School of Recruit Training.

I was at Innsworth for eight weeks, towards the end of which I attended two interviews. The officers concerned could not understand my removal from pilot training and their perplexity was relayed to me by an AC1 friend of mine who worked in Records. The AAU had to contribute personnel for guard duties, and on one occasion I was doing duty at the main gate (for five shillings: 25p.) for a friend who preferred to be in London at the time. An RAF vehicle turned in at the gate and several familiar faces looked down at me. The unsuccessful

members of my Digby course had arrived! The result of my interviews was selection for air gunnery training, and I was posted to the transit camp at RAF Driffield. With no immediate prospect of onward posting I was granted leave. The day after I arrived home I received a telegram: "Return to Driffield for posting". My destination was a few miles down the road at RAF Leconfield, my companions two failed pilot trainees, and we were to make up a course which consisted of several newly-qualified flight engineers who, as dictated by the policy of the time, had to complete the air gunners' course before promotion to Sergeant. The course was of eight weeks duration, shortened by the absence of drill periods. The flight engineers and ex-pilot trainees had already pounded the square and courses of National Servicemen coming directly to air gunnery training had spent six weeks doing their version of 'light foot drill' at RAF West Kirby.

Flying was in Lincoln bombers, and we were in one of the first courses to train in these aircraft. Until then ab initio air gunners flew in Wellingtons of 1938 basic design! Classroom subjects included the parts and operation of the turrets and guns plus the gyroscopic gunsight and aircraft recognition. Most of the instructors were SNCOs with an easy-going attitude, although sometimes tinged with resentment about National Servicemen who had no intention of making a career in the RAF. Flying consisted of air-to-air gunnery, using gunsight-mounted cine-cameras against Spitfires and occasionally and scaringly against fast jet fighters.

In August we were sent on leave and one of my ex-pilot trainee course-mates invited me to stay with his family in Maidstone. It was his birthday and his parents had bought him a car in which we would return to camp. In 1951 cars were virtually unobtainable, and it was lack of choice rather than finances which made them give him a second-hand BSA three-wheeler open top sports car. We drove up the A1, a different road in those days, and when approaching Yorkshire a cow crossed the road in front of a car towing a caravan which we were following. In avoiding the jack-knifed car/caravan in front, my friend drove up an embankment, having snapped a brake cable. We continued to Leconfield using the hand-brake only and resumed the course. One evening, after several pints in Beverley pubs, we returned to camp in the BSA — the brakes not repaired — and then had the idea of having a 'thrash' down the main runway. After reciting the Tiger Moth pre-take off check list at the end of the runway, we accellerated down the tarmac. The speedometer was registering 70 m.p.h. when the runway; we were on the short runway! We sped over the grass and went airborne over a wide stream, striking the opposite bank. I flew out, demolishing the windscreen with my left arm, and the driver followed, delayed by snapping the steering column with his stomach. The MO had to be called from a mess dinner to attend to my broken arm and I was despatched to Driffield hospital. Ten days later, I returned to be put on light duties, but it was found that a nerve in my arm had been severed and I was unable to extend the fingers of my left hand. Physiotherapy was arranged in Beverley hospital and while I was there one of the Lincoln aircraft sent from Leconfield to Jurby in the Isle of Man with our rugby team crash-landed on return, killing two of the team and injuring all the others on board. Being in the hospital, I was hailed as one of the unfortunate brave young men until the cause of my injury became clear, whereupon the atmosphere became quite chilly!

A strange spring-loaded device to allow me to use my fingers was fitted, and I completed the course classroom subjects. As I had now completed twelve months as an aircrew cadet I was awarded a special rate of pay, nearly £4 I believe. My name had been in an Admin. WRAF officer's card index for too long, and she demanded my posting. The Sqdn. Ldr. in charge of the Air Gunnery School asked me if I could fly with the strange device on my hand. Probably. Could I take it off long enough to attend the next passing-out parade and have the AG brevet pinned onto my chest? No problem.

So I became a Sergeant air gunner and went on leave. Returning to camp, I found I was posted to Coastal Command, which was illogical as I had insufficient service remaining in which to complete the training which would eventually lead to a Shackleton squadron. As I was not happy with the strapped-on hand, I requested an interview with the SMO, who had replaced the one who had attended to my injuries and who was unaware of my existence. The posting to Coastal Command was cancelled, an appointment at RAF Hospital Nocton Hall was arranged, and then a posting to the Medical Rehabilitation Unit at Headley Court in Surrey. There I received almost individual attention for six weeks, after which I returned to Leconfield with the use of my hand restored. I now had less than two months to the end of my service, and spent the time instructing on the Multiple Free Gunnery Trainer, which was situated in the corner of a hangar. I flew on air tests, checking the turrets of aircraft coming back into service after major overhaul, and walked many miles over Yorkshire in escape and evasion exercises.

On 7 February 1953 I handed in my flying gear, told the Station Warrant Officer I would not be available as mess barman and went home. My Sergeant's pay had been £6 per week plus £1 per week flying pay, with minimal mess charges, free clothing and much free travel. I turned down the two jobs on offer at the Labour Exchange and found myself a job in London at £6-4-0 (£6.20) per week.

❑ Mr. Jim R. Burton (2507750)

Although I was 'invited' to join the RAF, I had to defer the offer as I was an apprentice compositor in the printing trade, but after a two-year interval the offer came again and I dutifully made my way to RAF Padgate on 20 February 1951. There I was kitted out, but had a struggle with the beret, having always had an awkward-shaped size 7 5/8 head! The supplier said "If you can't get into that, try the fire bucket". I then managed to pull the beret on.

Next stop was RAF Weeton, near Blackpool, for a few weeks of being 'pulled into shape'. Looking back on that period, I was a fit 8 stone (I'm now 14 stone) and I made the best of it with trips into Blackpool (watching our polished brass go green in the breeze!) and walks around the villages between Blackpool and Weeton. On one of these occasions I met Reginald Dixon, organist at the Tower Ballroom, in a village church playing the organ, and as I was an aspiring organist we had an interesting session together!

After numerous injections — TABT, yellow fever, etc. — we were told we were going overseas. First stop was RAF Hednesford, where we spent a few weeks doing fatigues like picking stones off the lawn in front of the Sergeants' mess and placing them in buckets so that the duty Sergeant could throw them back on the lawn at night when he thought we weren't about, and painting white lines around the heaps of coal!

Then off to our destination — Egypt. Down to Southampton to join the troopship *Empire Ken,* a pre-First World War passenger liner once used by the Germans for pleasure cruises and still a nice ship. As there were only a few airmen on board, the army did all the chores! I joined the ship's band, playing piano, which got me out of many duties as I was practising! We stopped at Algiers, where we bartered from the ship and almost caused an international incident with our behaviour. Then on to Port Said, where we disembarked. After two weeks at sea we were glad to get onto dry (very dry) land again. There we boarded coaches for the trip to our next home, RAF Fayid.

our next home, RAF Fayid.

Settling down to life in that heat, we were told that we were to be R/T operators, as there was a shortage in Air Traffic Control. So straight in at the deep end, with 'on-the-job' training at a Master Diversion airfield. Initially working 24 hours on and 24 off, we soon learned our trade. After enough training, our teachers, mainly National Servicemen like us, left for home. Our new rota was 13.00 to 19.00 one day, 07.00 to 13.00 the next day, returning at 19.00 to work until 07.00 on the third day. We then a 'sleeping' day and a day off. We welcomed a wide range of aircraft over the months, including Yorks on trooping flights, Valettas of the two squadrons based at Fayid, Ansons, Proctors, Devons, a Canberra, and one or two civilian airliners when the airport at Cairo West was fogbound. Later we were introduced to Hastings aircraft and the civil counterpart, the Hermes. We had radio conversations with BOAC Comets on their South Africa trials and monitored the return journey from Kenya of our new Queen. On days off we were able to have some flights to such places as Aqaba, Entebbe and others whose names have since been changed.

Life on a busy airfield was far from boring! This was the year when Farouk was deposed as king of Egypt and the Egyptian Army set out to clear us from the Canal Zone. The nearest their soldiers came to us was about ten miles. All our guards were on the perimeter track, every second man with bullets in his rifle, while we sat in the control tower and never saw an Egyptian! They were frightened away by one of our Communications Flight Proctors; the pilot carried a pistol but otherwise no armour!

We left Port Said on our homeward journey on the troopship *Dilwara,* stopping at Malta for oil. Arriving at Southampton, we boarded a train to RAF

Lytham St. Anne's, the circle complete! There we had to walk from the station as all the RAF vehicles were busy on the East coast dealing with the terrible floods. I arrived home at 22.40 on 20 February 1953, my full two years of National Service over!

❏ Mr. Bob Dengel (2521739)

I started my National Service in July 1951 and because of the Korean War I was invited to apply to become aircrew. After reporting to RAF Padgate on 2 July I underwent two or three days of aircrew aptitude teats at RAF Hornchurch, and was classified as (1) pilot and (2) navigator. Between July and October I was given three months initial training at RAF Kirton-in-Lindsey, Lincolnshire, at the end of which I was selected to go to Canada to train as a pilot under the NATO scheme. In Canada I was commissioned as an Acting Plt. Off. I was stationed at RCAF Claresholm, Alberta, and trained on Harvard aircraft.

Early in 1952 we were paraded and informed of the death of King George VI and we then swore allegiance to HM Queen Elizabeth. By March I had received 20 hours dual instruction but had not yet managed to go solo. I then had a 'wash-out' check with the Chief Flying Instructor, in which my performance was not very good, and he said "If we put a chimpanzee in the cockpit and give him time he will solo — we haven't got that sort of time". He said that as my ground school marks were good I had two options — to go back to the UK or to go to navigation school in Winnipeg. I chose the latter!

After a spell of leave in Canada and the USA, during which I visited Vancouver, San Francisco, Los Angeles, Las Vegas etc., I went by rail to Winnipeg to join the Navigation School. I completed the course successfully and passed out in December 1952, and my commission as a Plt. Off.

"If we put a chimpanzee in the cockpit..."

was confirmed. I then returned home to the UK, in a Hastings from Montreal to RAF St. Eval, to where we were diverted due to a 'killer smog' at Lyneham!

In February 1953 I went on an acclimatisation course at RAF Lichfield, and there flew in Ansons and Valettas. There were still a few Wellingtons on the airfield, but I never flew in one. My training was at last finished, leaving me with four months service to do. I was posted to RAF Kinloss, a Coastal Command airfield in Scotland, where I worked in the operations room. I had occasional flights in Shackletons, on air tests, taking a crew to Cornwall to collect an aircraft, and taking 'top brass' to RAF Bovingdon for a conference in London. Exactly two years after reporting to Padgate, I was 'demobbed' and transferred to the RAFVR.

❏ Mr. F. A. Bird (3133796)

How strangely things work out! You see, I was originally due to enter the RAF in July 1951 but had earlier booked holiday with an aunt in Holland and this clashed with my call-up. At the time I was a member of a small-bore rifle club and one of its members worked in the office which sent out the call-up notices. With this man's assistance I made application for deferment in order to have my holiday, and hence did not join up until the August.

During my basic training at RAF Padgate I developed a septic toe caused by running in a cross-country race in service issue plimsolls, which shrank in the wet conditions. This put me in hospital for three weeks and I was re-Flighted.

On passing out I was posted to RAF Calshot, on Southampton Water, for marine craft training and on completion stayed there. Calshot had a full-bore rifle team, which suited me as I had been interested in shooting for about five years and I hoped I might make the RAF team at Bisley. The officer in charge was Flt. Lt. Hardyman, a good dedicated rifleman, and under him the team performed very well. I went on to make the Station team, Coastal Command team and the RAF team at Bisley as I had hoped. As usual, the inter-services shoot was held in July, and this is where things worked out in my favour, for if I had entered the Sevice in July as originally required I would have missed this great opportunity.

My surname, Bird, was sometimes was good for a laugh on morning parade when my name was called out and I was absent. Some smart alick would usually shout out "He's been night flying and hasn't returned". One amusing event I can remember was when our marine craft ferried a band back to the Isle of Wight and a crew member popped some fish into a bandsman's instrument case. The ensuing smell was apparently not located for some days!

At the end of my service, I was discharged as an LAC on 27 August 1953 and allocated to 61 Reserve Centre at RAF Kenley for Class H annual training.

❏ Wg. Cdr. R. I. Campbell (2531446)

My induction and medical was accomplished at High Wycombe in a large hall which was full of frantically busy people. There I had to make an instant decision about my future without consultation with my parents. "Did I want to train as aircrew" I was asked. I thought I might as well learn as much as possible while in National Service, so I agreed. I had no burning desire to fly nor an aeronautical background and had not been in the ATC. A 'job for life' had been selected for me by my father. I had two 'A' levels and eight 'O' levels, which was quite good in those days, and was an intellectual snob.

RAF Padgate, where I reported on 17 September 1951, was huge, and young men wandered about in various combinations of uniforms and civilian clothes. Aircrew volunteers were kept together. Each hut was supervised by an LAC or AC1 responding to the honorific "Staff" — I always found this weird. We had to buy our own cleaning materials etc., which caught some of us out as we had little money. Cleaning things — 'bull' — became and remained of over-riding importance for the next five months. Padgate food was lousy. Because of our upbringing, we were really very respectful of authority, and did what we were told and worried if we didn't. We were very bored most of the time, but we had detailed medicals, issues of kit, form-filling ad nauseam and drill in squads of 20 to 200. I don't recall my exact pay, but was able to save 3/6 (17.5p.) weekly in a Post Office account. I was very pleased with the colleagues I met here: our similar backgrounds helped us get on well quickly. Perhaps the following extract from a letter to my mother will give details of some aspects of Padgate life:

"Apart from the early morning, we manage to have a great many laughs..........about this early morning lark, it really is hellish waking up and then taking the plunge into the bitterly cold 6 a.m. air. Of course we are awakened by reveille played over the camp address system. These trumpet calls are preceded by a racket of record scratches, mike bangs and other atmospherics almost louder than the calls, which are played on a trumpet.......by someone with no teeth...........We heartily loathe it.........I shave the night before so as to have about five extra minutes under my nice warm blankets. Washing facilities here are excellent. Water is usually piping hot, and the baths are built for six-footers, and we can fill them as full as we like. But if you're unlucky all the hot water's been pinched and you have a tepid bath. We'd been on our feet all day, we'd collected all our webbing, been for lectures, had some drill, decorated the square for about an hour [I think I meant just stood around!] and had our uniforms inspected. My 'best blue' was badly creased when it was issued, and I had no time to press it, so the officer told me to do it. So I toddled down to the ironing room. There was a queue of about sixteen there, and two irons! I had to wait two hours to press my tunic".

We had to send our civilian clothes home; it was an offence to keep it, and I believe sending RAF stuff home for washing was another offence.

The mass of new impressions during that first week at Padgate made the week seem like a year. RAF Hornchurch, where I was sent on 27 September 1951, came as a sort of revelation. It had brick buildings, a fine NAAFI, and reasonable treatment from the staff. The aircrew medical impressed me with its thoroughness, and despite a cold (from the Padgate climate?) I was graded A1G1, and after a short interview I returned to Padgate on 2 October. We were now classified as 'static aircrew' while waiting for our Hornchurch results to come through. We marked time by cleaning things, collecting rubbish, drilling or standing on the square. I was given the task of painting '23' on identity discs because Flights were increasing in size. There were about 200 men in this sort of limbo, and the Padgate staff were hard-pressed to keep us occupied, as they had to keep us on camp.

On 10 October I was accepted as a pilot for two years' service. A Sqdn. Ldr. talked to us about signing on, telling us that he was paid £1405 p.a. at age 32, with 42 days' leave each year and a 48-hour and three 36-hour passes each month. I thought this was a pretty good deal but nobody in my group was tempted. Next day I was posted to RAF Digby for aircrew grading.

During our journey to Digby we changed stations in Manchester via a civilian bus — 44 of us, which must have impressed the citizens immensely! RAF Digby was comfortable, with grass round the brick billets, and trees and flowers. I lived in Room 4, Block 42. We were allowed freely off camp within one mile; trips further away had to be signed out at the guardroom. The free zone was no big deal, as there was nothing to do around Digby; a bus into Lincoln cost 2/6 (12.5p.) return. So everyone hitched; imagine Saturdays, with about a hundred men all with the same idea lining the roads! Food and NAAFI I classed as poor. Reveille here was at 06.30 and lights out at 22.30. The unit operated sixty Tiger Moths, and each cadet had twelve hours' flying, with tests at intervals.The staff were civilians employed by Airwork Ltd. 'Bull' remained strict, but there was less drill. We were told that 80% of us would go to Canada for flying training, but this turned out to be wrong — only a few navigators went in the end. At this time life was lived at a fast pace; everyone was firing off ideas and everyone was pursuing them. It was great fun!

On 15 October we were issued with flying kit — lambswool-lined suede boots with high heels (to stop feet slipping off the rudder bar); a huge sweater; gloves (silk inner, cape leather and long soft-leather gauntlets); a kapok-filled inner flying suit; an outer flying suit wired for electric heating; and a leather helmet with goggles and earpieces. I was surprised by the high quality of it all. After three days I was paid 18/- (90p.); any surplus over what we actually paid was accumulated and paid at the end of four months. I comment at this time that I was certainly NOT planning to take up the RAF permanently. It is true to say that we were building a genuine and pleasant sprit of camaraderie by this time, without jealousy or envy.

Once I lost my hat on the way back from Lincoln. Eventually I came up before the Sergeant SP, the Adjutant, and even the CO, to be lectured along the lines of "If you can't look after your hat, what chance have you with an aeroplane?" and was told to buy a new one. Digby was overcrowded, holding about twice as many cadets as built for. To ensure that every possible minute of favourable weather was used, we spent many hours on camp just waiting — nobody dared send us away for very long. I first flew on 25 October on straight and level flight and shallow turns. Apart from circuits, we did stalls and some aerobatics, and I began to get very enthusiastic about this flying business. As soon as batches of cadets finished at Digby, they were sent to 2 ITS, RAF Kirton-in-Lindsey, before the grading results were completed.

My time at 2 ITS was undoubtedly the most miserable time I ever had in the RAF. There I was a member of 1 Wing, 2 Squadron, 'B' Flight, and lived in Room 3, Block 40. Only our natural camaraderie and determination to do what we had set ourselves to do got us through those three months without defections. Looking back, I can see that the course was uncomfortable, unimaginative, geared to the level of the average 'brown job' squaddie and, all in all, a missed opportunity. Doubtless we learned something during the aviation-oriented lectures, but the admin., law, 'general duties' etc. were mugged up to pass a 'by rote' test and readily forgotten. The weather was no help: I have an over-riding impression of bitter cold, wind and rain outside and 'bull' to a senseless degree inside. Once I was told off for not cleaning my soapdish — it actually had soap on the inside! We scraped paint off hangar office floors with razor blades! I do NOT ascribe to the theory that this sort of nonsense is character-building in any positive sense. The officer training we received was pretty sparse and rather primitive; it is horrifying to think that we were going to be commissioned after this! Having run an OCTU Squadron in the late sixties, I now know how bad 2 ITS was.

The food at Kirton was good, but the NAAFI bad. I still relied heavily on food parcels from home! The regime was nit-pickingly strict, and one or two DIs positively enjoyed their short period of complete domination over young men soon to be their officers. The worst one, an evil little Irishman, was one we all wanted to meet again later, but I think he, wisely, left the Service.

On 2 December our grading results came through, pilots and navigators were separated, and I went with the pilots to Room 1, 'A' Flight. We underwent 'leadership' training: another cadet and I had to walk to Hibaldstow airfield and find out what it was being used for. We found Lincolnshire people very friendly to the RAF but their weather decidedly hostile. Then we had Exercise Magpie, in which we had to collect things — a sugar beet, the name of the last officer to sign out in the 48 book, a Sqdn. Ldr's doodle, a pub-owner's signature, a recent bus ticket to Scunthorpe, a pepper pot from the officers' mess, a pen from the guardroom and the name of the owner of the land to the east of the airfield! All without letting on that we were on an exercise! Soon we had progress tests, several inspections, and TABT jabs, and we were issued with officers' uniforms — four shirts, eight collars, socks, two pairs of shoes, a new battle-dress, a greatcoat and two berets. An allowance of £21 had to buy a raincoat (£18), gloves and cap (£3-10-0: £3.50). We were allowed to buy our already-issued kitbags and army-pattern boots (18/-: 90p.). The end of the course approached, with

final tests and interminable drilling, often in snow, for the passing-out parade on 28 January 1952. After the exams, we played sport, drilled twice daily for two hours at a time, and inevitably 'bulled'. When we broke ranks once, after yet more drill, to snowball the DIs, it wasn't the usual fun — we meant it! We went on a night evasion exercise in deep snow and frost but saw no-one despite lying quietly in the snow all night, and had a thoroughly useless and miserable time. Of course, it came to an end and we fled the place where we had been so fed up with no regrets at all.

After Kirton-in-Lindsey, we carried the rank of Plt. Off. on our serge battle-dress; we were actually Acting Plt. Off. (On Probation). We were commissioned on 7 February 1952, so were among the very first to be awarded a Queen's Commission rather than a King's. The probation lasted until we got our wings, I think, so we could be 'scrubbed' with the minimum of fuss.

I first went to 4 BFTS at Sywell, the airport for Northampton. We lived in bungalows designed to accommodate civilian passengers awaiting flights, and we were pretty comfortable. Flying training was done by civilians (all ex-RAF) employed by Airwork, with a small HQ unit to supervise us from an RAF point of view. The course was sixty hours, on

In May 1952, we progressed to 8 AFTS at Dalcross, the airport at Inverness. (Note how we NS trainees were trained at places hurriedly put into use). Here we had RAF instructors. The rush to get us trained was so intense that Oxford aircraft (twin-engined light transports) were de-inhibited from store at Kinloss to provide for our training, and pretty clapped-out old things they were too! Can you imagine training prospective fighter pilots (that was our aim — anyone who dropped out went to the other types of flying) on these? To me, it was always a grave disadvantage to have missed flying this critical stage of my training on Harvards. We stayed separate as National Service cadets until we went to our AFS (jet conversion to Vampires) and OCU (Vampires again), where we began to meet a few regulars, and we were then more or less in the main stream. At Dalcross, despite being classed as officers and living in an Officers' Mess (and wooden huts), we actually marched ourselves about in squads, being saluted en bloc by other ranks, and we were treated as really rather lower in status than a genuine AC2.

The panic speed of our training needs to be stressed. The Cold War was pretty frigid at the time, and Korea was in full swing. My training from enlistment to arriving on my first operational unit

(94 Sqdn. at RAF Celle in Germany) on 15 April 1953 was almost exactly eighteen months! I signed on for a four-year Short Service Commission soon after arriving on 94 (well, it WAS the most marvellous fun!), and eventually spent thirty-four and a half years in the RAF.

In my opinion, the RAF made a crucial error in commissioning all pilots and navigators. There were so many inexperienced, incompetent junior officers about that the officer status was degraded. If the RAF wished the serving conditions to tempt people to become aircrew, it would have been better done through pay adjustments and proper use of something like the Pilot 3, 2 and 1 and Master Pilot scheme. We were so fully occupied in learning our flying trade that we were almost all pretty ignorant about the other aspects of being an officer, and about the service outside our squadron, and couldn't have cared less! As National Service aircrew we had a degree of priority: it was scarcely 'status', but we were kept as a pack in the interests of forcing us through. The quality of training was not very good. Individual instructors were fine, but our programme left much to be desired. ITS was very bad — far too much drill and 'bull'; after all, we weren't aiming to beat the Brigade of Guards. BFTS at Sywell was fine, but the Oxfords at 8 AFTS at RAF Dalcross were brought into service purely in an effort to get us through in a hurry. Advanced training was pretty hit-and-miss, and it was left to the poor squadron guys to sort this mess out and start some real training when we came out of the 'sausage machine'.

❑ Mr. Richard Lee (2535123)

I think that what has to be remembered in my case is that I was an eighteen-year-old who had led a fairly sheltered life, living in a tiny village and working in the local town some four miles away. A visit to a cinema in this town was a highlight, with perhaps a glass of beer before catching the bus home. Village life centred around the church, the garden fête, and helping in our own large garden. In no way could I be called 'street wise' when I was recruited.

My service began on 16 October 1951, when I reported to RAF Padgate, a place I found very strange, with constant interruptions. The food was basic, but not like home cooking. I remember perhaps three dozen eggs all cooked at once in a large tray and then your portion was cut out of this block of eggs. There was plenty of food, and tea consisted of some cooked portion, perhaps fish, and then plenty of bread, margarine and jam with tea from the urns.

'Square-bashing' was at RAF Credenhill, near Hereford, to where we were sent in locked trains from Warrington. On arrival we were herded into lorries, with much shouting by the DIs. There was quite a lot of intimidation and a great deal of spit-and-polish. I remember lads sitting on their beds crying because they were homesick, lonely and perhaps frightened. We were living in wooden huts with a stove in the middle, but it was very cold at night, so everything went on the bed in an effort to keep warm. The outside toilet and bathroom blocks were freezing cold. Training was hard and discipline very strict, but we learned to cope and muttered under our breath, which I suppose relieved the tension somewhat. I particularly recall the gas chamber episode, when recruits were put inside for one minute with gas mask on, then moved around with mask off, then a further minute with it on before being allowed outside. Then came a 100-yard run before we could take the masks off. Much coughing and spluttering ensued and the rest of the day was free.

I was much happier at RAF Church Lawford, to where I was posted in January 1952 for trade training as a batman/waiter. I had worked as a clerk in civilian life, so I suppose this was suitable. There were wooden huts to live in, but much less 'bull'. Most of my time was spent as a waiter, working 72 hours on and 72 off. On the whole we were treated well, and I enjoyed working on dining-in nights. I was put in charge of the Officers' Mess bar, which I enjoyed as I had had the opportunity before recruitment of learning something about good food and drinks. There was quite a lot of noisy behaviour, and as an eighteen-year-old I remember being particularly shocked by a Sqdn. Ldr.'s wife who drank pints of bitter out of a mug! I also recall the officers singing all the verses of 'Green grow the rushes oh' as a drinking song and the Wg. Cdr. saying to me at 22.00 "Lee, close the bar now" and immediately the adjutant saying "Lee, don't go away" so that the bar could be re-opened as soon as the CO and his lady had left.

As my father died in March 1953, I applied for and got a compassionate posting to RAF Hemswell, which was much nearer my home. This was an active flying Station of Bomber Command and very different from Church Lawford. There were brick-built living quarters and better conditions, but when I arrived I was issued with a .303 Enfield rifle, which I had not handled since my 'square-bashing' days. It was presumably for use in an attack of some kind, but I have to admit it went into the armoury store and stayed there until I left the service. The runways and aircraft were strictly out of bounds except to those flying or working on the aircraft, so we only saw the Lincolns and Canberras from a distance.

The Officers' Mess had a civilian mess secretary, who treated us as a sergeant-major would have done, and there was a lot less companionship. Again I worked 72-hour shifts, and remember sitting in the mess kitchen with the duty cook in the early hours of the morning waiting for the first aircraft to return from practice bombing raids. It would be about 30 minutes from the first aircraft landing to the arrival of its crew for breakfast. Then pots of tea had to be ready and breakfast of eggs, bacon, toast etc. was served. The crews looked very tired but were always very polite to me and welcomed their meal.

For a couple of weeks I worked for the CO, a Gp. Capt. with a distinguished war record, in his home. Both he and his wife treated me kindly and his various uniforms and decorations made quite a lasting impression on me, a 20-year-old.

In May 1953 I was sent to RAF Uxbridge as a waiter at the time of the Coronation of the present Queen, to help look after the high-ranking officers drafted in for the parade. We worked very hard, and as a treat were allowed to stand at the back and watch the concert being presented by the 'Stargazers', a popular singing group at the time.

I left the RAF in October 1953 and was not sorry. I am the first to admit that the experience did me a lot of good, but I was not the type to make a career in the Service.

❏ Mr. David Evans (2536336)

My service number was 2536336 and I joined on 24 October 1951 at RAF Padgate. On the way there, at Cardiff, I met a chap who became 2536335, and I'm pleased to say we've remained friends ever since. After a week's induction and kitting out we proceeded by train and truck to 11 School of Recruit Training at RAF Hednesford for eight weeks 'squarebashing'. I'm afraid I found the first six weeks very hard and service life very difficult to adjust to. However, in the last week of training about four of us in the billet were informed that we were to be telegraph assistants and were on draft for the Middle East.

We left Hednesford on 2 January 1952 and proceeded on fourteen days' leave. This passed very quickly and I travelled overnight on the 15th to arrive at 5 Personnel Despatch Unit at RAF Lytham St. Anne's by 06.00 next morning. Lytham I can only decribe as chaotic, and it was rumoured that one or two people had spent their two years there [awaiting embarkation]. The bane of our existence was one Cpl. Register, who used to roam the camp drumming up recruits for fatigues. Known to all and sundry as George, he was a real character. The highlights were a trip to Blackpool and every weekend the long journey home on a 48-hour pass, which included the delights of a four-hour stop at Crewe on the way back. After some weeks, all four Telegraph Assistants were told that we not going overseas after all and were formed into a Pool Flight to await home postings as trainee telephonists. We had just settled into our new billet when someone opened the door one morning and announced "George is dead". Thinking it was the unfortunate Cpl. Register, we began to cheer, but then it became clear that it was King George VI.

We left Lytham on 16 February 1952 on posting to RAF Wattisham in Suffolk. I can recall crossing Manchester by bus and only having a short time to make our connection, when the bus shuddered to a stop. Needless to say we began discussing the reasons for the delay when a rather formidable elderly lady in front gave us a real ticking-off. It transpired that there was a two-minutes silence for the King's funeral. After another nightmare journey we arrived at Wattisham, which we found to be a permanent pre-war Station with good facilities compared with what we had encountered previously. It was a three-squadron fighter Station with a Group Captain as Commander. When I met the Station Signals Officer his first question was "Evans, are you Welsh?". "Yes sir". "Do you play Rugby?". "No sir". "I'm sorry, we've no room for you here, you're posted". Hey presto, on the Friday I was on my way to RAF Church Fenton in Yorkshire, while my non-Rugby-playing English colleagues remained at Wattisham! Needless to say, the Station Signals Officer was Welsh and was the Station Rugby Officer.

Church Fenton was also a fighter Station but with only two squadrons and a Wing Commander, I. S. Smith, as Station Commander. It seems that he won the DFC on Mosquitos during the war. He was known as Black Smith on account of his Maori extraction and was a very strict man and a keen disciplinarian. Station Routine Orders were known as 'Blacksmith Blues' after a hit tune of the period.

The Conservatives had returned to power on the second day of my service, and Churchill had the idea that the Russians would stage a mass parachute invasion. He was not having thousands of RAF men idling about, so we spent quite a few March nights/early mornings on the bleak Yorkshire moors waiting for army parachutists who never seemed to appear. All this was coupled with the not too arduous task of training as a telephonist and frantic preparation for an AOC's inspection at the end of March. The AOC was AVM Sir Richard

Atcherley, one of the famous twins of that rank. The inspection went very well, and I completed my training by 24 April, which meant that my pay rose to the dizzy height of 5/6 (27.5p.) per day with the rank of AC1.

At the beginning of May a colleague and I were sent on a 28-day detachment to Orby, a small radar establishment near Skegness. The Station was used as a training school by some 100 Marconi personnel, as that company had secured an Air Ministry contract. There were 25 RAF personnel commanded by Flt. Lt. Ted Murray: one Flt. Sgt., 8 RAF police and 15 airmen. As the camp had no fresh water supply we all lived in civilian boarding houses. Flt. Lt. Murray was a really nice chap who promised to do his best to extend our stay, and he was as good as his word, as I eventually stayed ten and a half months and my colleague over a year. As Skegness was a holiday resort, but with a fairly short season, we had plenty of entertainment. Our working day was relatively easy, the only drawback being the shortage of cash. We integrated well into the life of the town and I played soccer for a local club, courtesy of the sports-mad Flt. Sgt. The sad news of Marconi's departure came at Christmas, and it seemed that the end was in sight. By this time I had reached the dizzy height of SAC and was receiving 8 shillings (40p.) per day. The only remaining highlight was the East Coast floods in February 1953. We volunteered to help, and spent a very wet night rescuing people from flooded houses in the village of Ingoldmells. Came 18 March and I personally took the signal ceasing my detachment because I was posted to Shipton.

I left Skegness with a lot of regret on 22 March and returned to Church Fenton. There I learned that RAF Shipton was a brand new underground Sector Operations Centre near York, and I would live at RAF Linton-on-Ouse. Thus with seven months remaining I joined my last unit. It was like enlisting again after my easy life at Skegness, but I soon got used to the more irksome facets of life, such as working parades, queues for food and in the NAAFI, booking in and out of camp etc. The work and working conditions were good, and being in Signals and a shift-worker I usually got away with murder! For the last six months I was on regulars' pay of 11 shillings (55p.) per day, so I was relatively well off. At Shipton the Signals Officer was Fg. Off. Pickering, an extremely fair man, and the SWO was Warrant Off. Preston, who had a fine voice and who was a keen disciplinarian, but his bark was far worse than his bite.

All in all the last six months passed very quickly, and I was 'demobbed' on 23 October 1953. To be fair, I enjoyed my National Service after the first six months. I found it very difficult to settle down in 'Civvie Street' and re-enlisted in July 1956.

☐ Mr. Robert Owen (2540306)

After catching a train from my home town, Kidderminster, I found myself at Crewe, where I was joined by many other 'lost' individuals, all carrying suitcases. On arrival at Warrington we were all herded onto lorries and driven to RAF Padgate, where at about 5.00 p.m. we had our first RAF meal, a plate of rabbit stew!

Kitting-out at Padgate took about ten days, after which I was sent to RAF Innsworth, just outside Gloucester, for eight weeks' initial training, which was not a very nice experience. When the eight weeks had been completed and the passing out parade was over, the postings for trade training were announced. I found that I was the only one from my intake to be chosen for the RAF Regiment, the army of the RAF. After leave, I made my way to RAF Dumfries in Scotland for eight weeks of small arms training—rifle, Bren, Sten and drill again. The train left Birmingham for Glasgow at 11.00 p.m. and arrived at Carlisle, where I had to change trains, at 6.00 a.m. next day. A porter at Carlisle told us that the King was dead.

RAF Dumfries was a disused wartime airfield and living conditions were not very good. The water was cold, the huts were concrete, there was a shortage of fuel and food and a cold, raw, wind blew every day. At the end of the eight weeks the course was split up; some lads went to RAF Weeton for eight weeks driving instruction, some to RAF Compton Bassett to learn signals, and one or two to RAF West Kirby on an armourers' course, but most went to RAF Watchet in Somerset for eight weeks' training on 40mm. light anti-aircraft guns. At the end of the course we took some leave and then were posted to RAF Hawarden, where we met some of the other lads who had been at Dumfries with us. We reached Hawarden a few at a time and were told that we were to form 75 LAA Squadron, RAF Regiment. At first there were no NCOs, but before long a couple of Sergeants and the CO arrived. He told us that we would be going to RAF Luneberg in West Germany.

After a few weeks we left Hawarden for Harwich by rail, all kitted out, caught the boat to the Hook of Holland, then travelled by train again to Luneburg, near Hamburg. This was a former Luftwaffe station and there were many empty centrally-heated barrack blocks. For the first few weeks we had no guns or Corporals, but soon six guns arrived for each Flight, some of our own men were trained to become Corporals, and the full complement of officers arrived. When 80 LAA Squadron arrived and were housed nearby the two units became 25 Wing RAF Regiment.

Early in 1953 25 Wing was posted to a new RAF Station, as yet not completed, near the Dutch border — RAF Geilenkirchen. After a while the airfield became operational, and Sabre jet fighters and a squadron of Belgian Air Force Thunderjets arrived. Gun pits were dug around the airfield and many exercises were held. In June 1953 25 Wing took part in the Coronation Parade at Dusseldorf with the Coldstream Guards, the Royal Marines and the Black Watch, for which we trained for two weeks at Bradbury Barracks, Krefeld.

In November 1953, the National Service members of the squadron — most of us — began to drift away, our two years almost completed. I and three or four others were sent to RAF Lytham St. Anne's for 'demob'. Within a few days service life was at an end — a job well done.

❏ Mr. R. S. Gorringe (2545053)

As I had been serving an apprenticeship, my call-up came three days after my 21st birthday, on 21 January 1952. Arriving at Euston Station, I was confronted by chaps in assorted dress with attaché cases, some jolly, some concerned, all awaiting the train to Warrington. As the train sped north, we noticed snow getting ever thicker as we continued our journey — all rather depressing! On arrival at Warrington we were greeted by RAF police, all bellowing at our motley crew to form up and march to the lorries waiting outside the station.

When we arrived at RAF Padgate, we were rather alarmed to observe what appeared to be a prison camp. We were herded to a reception centre, asked if we could speak Russian, issued with our 'irons', given a mug of tea and taken to a reception billet. Then we were marched to the cookhouse and lined up for our first meal. This consisted of a piece of cheese, an onion, lettuce leaves and beetroot soaked in vinegar. So appalling was it that a chap promptly deserted! In the 'Daily Mirror' a few days later was a headline "Recruit who didn't stay for tea" or words to that effect. The police later picked him up in London.

The following week was a generally easy time, spent being kitted out and cleaning the billet while we waited for our 'square-bashing' postings. These came all too soon, and to my disgust I was to stay at Padgate. Those of us staying were marched over to the Wings, our kitbags on our shoulders, in a snowstorm. On arrival we were confronted by a frightfully smart Corporal DI who immediately started bellowing at us. We were now part of 8 Flight. What a bleak place the hut which was to be our billet looked, with rows of beds on which were three 'biscuits' that acted as mattresses. The first job was to fill in a card giving the name of our next of kin. That evening, having collected our bedding and been taught how to set it out in RAF fashion, we were instructed how to attach our webbing etc.

Next day 'square-bashing' really started, with drill, rifle drill, and slow marching to the tune of 'Over The Sea To Skye', whistled by ourselves. As it was winter, PT was a real laugh, with blokes lined up wearing PT kit — vest and shorts — covered by our overcoats, with socks, and boots with the tabs sticking out! What a sight! It was so cold that winter that the ablution blocks, detached from the billets, froze up. There were queues at the sinks, with a dribble of water from the tap for our shave at 06.00.

At night we stoked up the two cast iron stoves in the billet until they glowed cherry red. In the morning our small kit, flannel, soap etc., which was kept in a box at the foot of our beds, was frozen to the box, it was so cold. My room job was to black-lead the stoves before breakfast each morning. For three weeks our days consisted of drill, ground combat training, and the assault course, on which our highly-polished boots got soaked in water and mud, but were expected to be shining for parade next morning. Friday afternoon was always the CO's parade, and Wg. Cdr. A. Blackwell-Smythe took the salute as we marched past to the tune 'Sussex By The Sea'.

One morning we were lined up on parade when all those of 6'0" and over in height were ordered to step forward. We were to be re-Flighted to 13 Flight to be trained to line the route of a Trooping The Colour parade to be held in Manchester for King George VI. For this we were issued with 'cheese-cutter' caps, probably one of the first units in the RAF to receive them. 13 Flight was a 'spit-and-polish' Flight; all we did every day was drill, route marching (which gave us blisters from our new boots) and ground combat training. However, the King died, and we were sent back to 8 Flight. We then had nerve-gas lectures and a spell in a hut filled with tear gas, when we had to remove our gas masks for a time, giving us roaring headaches later. Two day after receiving our jabs, in pain and not feeling too well, we were marched to the camp cinema to see the American film on VD. It was very explicit, and about five people collapsed sideways off their seats.

The next step was our exams, after which we

would be graded. Those with the highest marks would be considered for the top five trades — engine mechanic, airframe mechanic, etc. I managed to get home the weekend before passing-out parade, which was to be on a Monday afternoon. I went to my own barber and asked him to cut my hair short. After returning to camp, we were paraded for inspection before the passing-out parade that afternoon. I was ordered to get another haircut! I was really surprised and impressed how smart we all looked on this parade, and in only eight weeks. However, through being re-Flighted, our postings were late in arriving, so we spent another two weeks 'square-bashing', which made us super-fit at the end, and rather proud.

Our postings came through, and I was to be an airframe mechanic (rigger) so off I went to RAF St. Athan in South Wales. St. Athan in the summer was like a holiday camp after Padgate. We started a twelve-week intensive course, which consisted of lectures on hydraulics, pneumatics, RAF documents, theory of flight, technical drawing, corrosion, dis-similar metals, practical workshop and aircraft marshalling. This last consisted of visiting the runway, where a Warrant Oficer piloted an Auster along the track while the airman on the tarmac in front gave him instructions with the bats. The pilot, however, thought he'd have some fun, and accellerated the aircraft towards the batsman, the propellor coming ever closer as he ran backwards!

The only snag at St. Athan was the RAF police. Their first posting after training at RAF Pershore was there, and they were dead keen. We had to pass the guardroom to reach our billets, and would stand around until about six 'erks' had gathered, line up and march to the guardroom. The idea was that there was safety in numbers, and there was less likelihood of being picked on for any small infringement of dress!

On 48-hour passes, we would club together and book a coach to White City, or take the train. The return journey by train meant that we arrived at St. Athan at 06.00 and had one hour in bed and had to try to keep awake during a day of lectures.

The course finished and we lined up on the square, where a Warrant Oficer told us that we would all be on the boat to the Far East, and that meant Korea! Two days later, we all received home postings! I was posted to RAF Bassingbourn, in Cambridgeshire. Six of us arrived at the guardroom in the evening, were given a scratch meal and told to find beds for ourselves as the camp was full. I found a bed in the Fire Section, and was just dozing off when I was rudely awakened by a big black Yank

who wanted to sell me his ration of Camel fags because he was short of cash. This was a regular feature of the time. It was strange being stationed alongside the Americans. We would march to work in the hangars while they rode by on motorcycles smoking fat cigars and taking the mickey out of us.

At first, work in the hangar was second-line servicing on Mosquitos, Meteors and Canberras. On one occasion, SAC Dix, sitting in the cockpit of a Mosquito, selected 'undercarriage up' by mistake and screamed "Get out, get out" to those of us who were standing underneath. Luckly, the safety locks didn't break. I went to work in the hydraulics bay, where I specialised in overhauling the Dunlop disc brakes fitted to the Canberras. These aircraft were being grounded because the brake-pads kept falling off. I selectively fitted pads using rivets left behind by the Americans, and Bassingbourn was the only Station that didn't have grounded Canberras due to brake problems. This meant kudos for all concerned.

When the time came for me to be 'demobbed' the Squadron Leader and Wing Commander i/c Technical Wing invited me to their office and thanked me for what I had done, accompanied by snide remarks from my mates!

❏ Mr. Michael Wood (2551035)

In February 1952 I reported to RAF Padgate, taking with me personal small kit such as toothbrush, toothpaste and a hairbrush, to buy which I had been sent the sum of 4 shillings (20p). After kitting-out I was sent to RAF Hednesford for basic training. On the wall of each billet hut was a large chart showing how the full array of RAF kit was to be displayed for inspection. My bunk was next to the chart and thus I was the first to be inspected. I had a hairbrush of my own which I had taken to Padgate and stamped with my new service number as we were told to do with the RAF-issue brushes. This I placed with my kit in its correct place, although the chart must have been out of date as hairbrushes were no longer issued. When the Station Warrant Officer (otherwise known as God!) and the Corporal i/c the billet began checking he saw my brush, checked the chart, and, finding that nobody else was displaying a hairbrush, told the Corporal to take all their names and order them to go out and buy one! I was not very popular for a time after this episode!

In May 1952, after basic training, I was posted to RAF Manston as a clerk/EA. Other airmen in the same Flight were sent to more romantic places like Aden, Singapore or Gibraltar. The questions were

— what is a Clerk/EA and where is Manston? I soon foundout that I was supposed to be an Equipment Accountant and that Manston was near Ramsgate in Kent. As I had never been south of London this was all going to be very exciting; after all, Manston was in Fighter Command, the most prestigious Command of all, in 11 Group, and names like Bader, Stanford Tuck and Dizzy Allen sprang to mind.

Travelling by train to Ramsgate, the person sitting opposite me had a paper with headlines stating Another Manston Thunderjet Crash. Another? And what was a Thunderjet? At that time I didn't know that Manston was a USAF operational Station and was surprised when I learnt later that there were several thousand Americans there and only 250 or so RAF personnel.

I did all the arrival checks and was allocated a very old double-deck bunk in hut E.15, which still had some enemy machine-gun bullet holes in it. These huts had at one end the Corporal's room and at the other the toilet and a room for the cleaning materials. All wash and bath facilities were some way over the road in a 'field' opposite, which was fine until it rained, when it became a sea of mud.

On reporting to the section which I now knew to be the Equipment Provisioning & Accounting Section, I was greeted by Sgt. Whiffen, a most amiable individual of very long service, with the comment "What, not another trainee — are you sure you're supposed to be here?" The section was at the time heavily over-manned, though this was to change later. Following the usual exchange of names and greetings I was shown round and told that on the next day, 21 May, we were invited to a show being put on by the USAF in their Thunderjets as a morale booster after several crashes. We all duly appeared on the airfield on a bright sunny day. The jets streaked by, watched by the entire Station, including the wives of the pilots. Yes, the inevitable happened, a crash, seen by us all. Over forty years later, I can still see the orange/yellow glow on the other side of the control tower. I believe our own Gp. Capt. Jamie Rankin was first on the scene as I seem to remember an order coming in for a new uniform for him.

As I was a clerk I should have been on the roster for 'duty clerk', but as there was an acute shortage of storemen we had to fulfil the latter role. This mainly meant turning up at 06.00 to a little hut near the MT Section so as to be able to unlock the petrol pumps, check the 'dips' and then await the vehicles for refuelling, which never arrived before 07.55, just as the duty was coming to an end. Having sat there in the winter in the freezing cold for nearly two hours, I actually welcomed the activity. It was worse if one

was landed for this duty on a Bank Holiday. Yes, my turn came round, in August 1952 I believe it was, and I spent four whole days manning the pumps and being on call for the occasional vehicle to fill up. I was told we never had an aircraft in for refuelling over an August grant period. Well, there's always a first time. This August came the largest RAF exercise seen in the south-east, lasting the full four days of the grant. I was very soon called out by the duty MT driver, who arrived in a very excited state saying that there was a whole squadron of Meteors to refuel. Fortunately he knew what to do and we were soon down at the section collecting all the keys and distributon books. I had to fill a large bowser with AVTAG, and I recall the driver was going to connect the hose from the bowser to the tanks, but somehow with the roar of the Meteors overhead we omitted to do so and the next thing I knew someone was shouting that there was fuel flowing down the road to Birchington-on-Sea! The fire section came out and neutralised the effect. I now had to account for several hundred gallons of fuel, and by some devious method I was able to 'adjust' the records in the section and at the tanks so that the figures agreed. In fact I was congratulated on the excellence of the deliveries of fuel I'd made over the holiday period! My thanks to those drivers who unwittingly signed for fuel they did not receive!

Like most RAF Stations, we had an Astra Cinema. Ours was run by a Mr. G. P. Moorhouse, a civilian who resided in the Sergeants' mess. Staff were recruited from the RAF personnel, mainly from EPAS, and very soon I was offered employment in the evenings at 3 shillings (15p.) per night for tearing tickets in half and stopping people coming in through the exit door at half time. We had two shows each night, with some very good films. I remember seeing 'Genevieve' some 32 times, as the work only lasted about twenty minutes each performance. In between, you could watch the film or pop over to the NAAFI for a game of snooker or whatever. Promotion soon followed, and I was selling ice creams at 3/9 (19p) a night, followed by the ultimate promotion, to cashier at six shillings (30p.) a night, which bearing in mind that the RAF paid an SAC eleven shillings (55p.) per day was very good as an extra. I was probably the only person on the Station who could change the US scrip money into sterling, as we had two sets of tickets — 1/6 and 20 cents. Scrip could not be used by the RAF personnel as it was only valid in the Post Exchange stores, but various deals took place in both currencies. Later, the USAF took over the cinema, making us all redundant and putting in their own staff.

On Thanksgiving Day we were usually invited to attend the celebrations and very much enjoyed the USAF hospiality, especially the blueberry pie and the turkey. Other memories of Manston which come to mind include Taff's Café, the Acacia Café, the bookies' runner, and the Jolly Sailor. No account of this Station would be complete without mention of the SWO — Warrant Officer Allcock, feared by all but well-meaning and fatherly. I'm certain he actually varnished his boots! I'm pleased that there is a photo of him in the Spitfire Museum. On a more serious note was the event involving a coloured USAF airman which took place shortly after I left Manston. At about the spot in Halley Road where I used to walk to collect the post each morning at 09.00, he apparently went berserk, and with a carbine in hand fired at all and sundry, killing three people and injuring about ten. There but for the grace of God go I!

❏ Mr. G. R. Leftwich (2555724)

I am enclosing photo-copies of my discharge papers, from which you will note that I did not receive any training other than basic. I first went to RAF Padgate for kitting-out and then to RAF Hednesford for eight weeks 'square-bashing'. Never before or since had I been so perfectly fit. We had a celebrity with us: Michael Korda, nephew of the famous Korda brothers, the film makers, a nice bloke. During this period films were very popular and to have someone talking about film stars he had met, without any boasting, was very enjoyable.

Before call-up, I had been a telegraphist earning £4-4-0 (£4.20) a week with Cable & Wireless and was familiar with Morse code. However, I failed a sound test and was sent to RAF Kidlington, the home of the Oxford University Air Squadron, as a storeman at £1-8-0 (£1.40) a week. Soon after I arrived, there was a shortage of teleprinter operators, so I remustered on the spot. I must have been a very rare breed in that I spent the rest of my time in the RAF in Signals without any formal training, but I could do the job as I had been trained for eighteen months by C&W in the full range of telegraphy.

❏ Mr. E. Caton (2576583)

Twenty conscripts who gathered at Southend-on-Sea on a July day in 1952 had all opted to do their National Service in the RAF. I was fortunate to be one of only two selected; the other young man had arrived in the uniform of an ATC Flt. Sgt.

On a wet Monday, 3 November 1952, I arrived at RAF Padgate to become AC2 Caton E. A fellow recruit was half-way through marking his kit when it came to light that two digits had become transposed in the service number allocated to him. After the inevitable panic had subsided, it was decided his number couldn't be changed, and thus two National Servicemen bore the number 2567562.

At RAF Hednesford I spent a miserable ten weeks or so in appalling weather. 'Square-bashing', happily interrupted by Christmas leave, was followed by a spell on Pool Flight supervising the issue of coke from the compound. Many and devious were the ruses employed by recruits to scrounge extra fuel: I turned a blind eye to all of them. After all, I'd been a recruit a week or two earlier, snow was falling and it was freezing! At my trade selection interview I resisted blandishments to train as a service policeman and expressed an interest in becoming a photographer, only to be told that I would need to sign on for eight years, and even that would offer no guarantee of becoming a photographer. As I had learned to type and write shorthand in my civilian job I was sent to RAF Credenhill, Hereford, to be trade-tested as a shorthand-typist. Only modest standards were required for promotion to LAC; I passed easily and was promoted (and paid) retrospectively to my enlistment date.

Although I hoped to be posted to a flying Station near my Essex home I was sent to RAF Norton, near Sheffield, the small parent unit for a travelling Ground Radar Servicing Squadron. As the only shorthand writer, I acted as secretary to the CO, Wg. Cdr. Kenneth Mummery, in addition to my routine typing duties, and acted as clerk to his weekly conference. His regular morning parades culminated in the raising of the RAF flag and his departure from the parade ground into SHQ via his personal entrance. On one occasion, I had been in SHQ as duty clerk from an early hour, and having 'bulled' the area inside the CO's entrance, had locked the door to prevent illegal entrance. Unfortunately, I'd forgotten to unlock it! The CO marched up to his door as usual, failed to open it, and had perforce to suffer the indignity, before almost the entire Station complement, of walking round to enter by the other ranks' door. "Charge the duty clerk", instructed the CO, but the charge was dropped when it became clear that I was the culprit, as he would have been deprived of his secretary if I had been given 'jankers'.

I didn't like Sheffield and wasn't contented with my lot at RAF Norton. There was little to relieve the monotony, and the prospect of completing my two years' service there was bleak. So in July 1953 I broke the cardinal rule by volunteering for a posting to SHAPE (Supreme HQ Allied Powers Europe), the military HQ of NATO, located at Versailles, near Paris. Possibly because a typist rather than a shorthand-typist was required, I was not accepted, but a week or two later I was offered the chance of a posting to HQ AAFCE (Allied Air Forces Central Europe), also in France. So it was that at the end of August, the first member of my immediate family to venture abroad, I found myself at Camp Guynemer in the Forest of Fontainebleu, home not only to the RAF but also the air forces of Belgium, Canada, France, Holland and the USA.

A far cry from a normal RAF Station, the domestic side of the camp and the HQ building from which it was separated by a public road were of modern construction, purpose-built by NATO. 'Erks' were billeted four to a room in centrally-heated two-storey blocks, two of which were allocated solely to the RAF and one shared with the Dutch contingent. The RAF had its own mess, but the Dutch had opted to share with the RCAF and USAF in the latter's 'chow hall'. Belgians shared the French mess. The usual RAF practice of taking mugs and 'irons' to and from the mess ended when it was realised that this appeared undignified to the other nations' airmen. Thereafter, tables for four were laid with cups, saucers and cutlery and a Corporal mess orderly was appointed. Unheard of luxury, indeed!

Each of the six air forces had its own support unit, and I was assigned to that of the RAF, principally to look after the English-language lending library in the Education Officer's office. A few weeks later, having been security-cleared to the highest level, I was transferred to the HQ building and the office of the Commander, the legendary Sir Basil Embry KCB KBE DSO + 3 bars DFC AFC. I was to replace the SAC who I think was the only other shorthand-typist on the strength, who had elected to transfer to the RCAF and emigrate. The personal staff of Sir Basil, who had taken over command only the previous July, were all RAF personnel, and he would have it no other way. Office staff comprised Sqdn. Ldr. George Lewis (Personal Staff Officer); Flg. Off. Robin Lees (Aide-de-Camp); long-serving Wt. Off. Fred Custance (Secretary); Sgt. Stan Fenny (Clerk); and myself (deputy Secretary and general dogsbody). I count myself fortunate to have worked with men like these. Sqdn. Ldr. Lewis increasingly became something of a surrogate father to me. Flg. Off. Lees, the son of Air Marshal Sir Alan Lees, represented the RAF at tennis, squash and hockey and in the 1980s attained Air rank himself.

Welshman Sgt. Fenny, as a Flt. Lt., had been the navigator and sole survivor of a crashing Halifax late in the War, and successfully evaded capture. Having left the RAF, he soon applied to rejoin but was not permitted to regain his commission.

The office establishment allowed for an additional Corporal clerk, but there was not enough work to justify filling the vacancy. Normally, Sir Basil dictated his letters to Wt. Off. Custance, who re-dictated the less important items to me. Our very early IBM electric typewriters then came into their own. Much of my share of the dictation related to the work of the RAF Escaping Society, of whom Sir Basil was then Chairman. On occasions when he dictated to me direct he would ask when he had finished "Is that all right?" — this from the man who, as AOC 2 Group, had flown his Mosquito on tree-top-level daylight attacks on targets in occupied Europe!

Sir Basil was not too happy about certain aspects of the NATO situation and was also concerned about some of the conditions to which RAF personnel were subject, especially when compared with those of their colleagues in the other air forces, e.g. pay, allowances, and uniforms. He made himself somewhat unpopular by making noises in high places, with the result that he was required to retire early from the Service. Included in those 'high places' was Royalty in the form of HRH the Duke of Edinburgh, who visited AAFCE in the summer of 1954. The Duke arrived in the uniform of Admiral of the Fleet, and Flg. Off. Lees accepted the proffered gold-encrusted cap, which, after the Duke had disappeared into the private office, was plonked upon my head by one of the officers. I've often speculated on the offences with which I could have been charged; impersonating an officer or a Duke? In attendance was the Central Band of the RAF, and I was astonished by the scruffy appearance of the bandsmen's uniforms when seen at close quarters. The present-day uniforms are a far cry from those of 1954, when they were little better than standard 'best blues'.

One day in December 1953 I found myself in a USAF staff car, together with an RCAF Flt. Sgt. from the Chief of Staff's office, travelling in convoy on an exercise designed to test the ability of the HQ to transfer to its designated wartime location and to send a message to 2nd TAF in Germany mobilising them to intercept a Russian attack. In the boot of the car was an empty crate simulating my typewriter and stationery. The Official Secrets Act probably prevents me saying where we were bound for; suffice it to say that it was in the Paris area and proved to be the secret underground HQ constructed during the War for Hitler's use when directing Operation Sealion, the invasion of the British Isles. Hitler's own vast office would be used by Sir Basil. My office, a small concrete cell at the far end of the corridor leading to Hitler's, contained only a small table on which I placed my empty crate. Not much happened after that, although later I learned that we had been annihilated after two minutes! We weren't allowed to return home until we had endured a night in cockroach-infested billets with straw palliasses and canvas sheets, shaving outside in cold water and, the ultimate indignity, a British army field kitchen.

Christmas was upon us, and four days after returning to Camp Guynemer I flew to RAF Bovingdon, Hertfordshire, in an Anson piloted by Air Commodore Peter Wykeham-Barnes DSO OBE DFC AFC, who was in charge of the Operations Directorate at HQ AAFCE. This trip was in part due to the kind efforts of Sqdn. Ldr. Lewis and partly to my position in the Commander's office. The Communications Flight was based about fifteen miles from Camp Guynemer, at Melun/Villaroche. As well as two or three Ansons, Sir Basil's personal Devon or Pembroke was based there. I was fortunate to fly home several times in each aircraft and to fly in March 1954 to Nice for an overnight stay. That time, in case of awkward questions, I carried a sealed envelope containing two blank sheets of paper, addressed to Sir Basil and endorsed SECRET — BY HAND. Sir Basil met the aircraft at Nice and greeted me with "Hello Clayton" (he never did get my name right!). All my flights were in the nature of 'gash flips' necessitating signature of the 'blood chit' absolving everybody from HM the Queen downwards of any liability in the event of injury to my person. Never once did Sir Basil question my presence on an aircraft; not many 'erks' can boast of being flown by an Air Chief Marshal!

It came to Sir Basil's notice that the food in the RAF airmen's mess was not all it might have been, so one teatime he paid a surprise visit. Only I knew what was afoot. The consternation among the cooks, resplendent in their filthiest 'whites' and wearing their most ridiculous hats, was a joy to behold. I don't suppose any of them had ever set eyes on so much 'scrambled egg' and 'fruit salad' adorning the uniform of one individual. The catering officer was not present and the can had to be carried by, I believe, a Sergeant. "Any complaints?". Sir Basil approached every table except the one where I sat. Nobody said a word. Next morning Sir Basil sought my opinion of the meal (toad in the hole) and asked why he had received no response in the mess. As I

could only suggest that the airmen were probably intimidated by an officer of such high rank and by the presence of the catering Sergeant, half a dozen airmen were collared at random and asked their views in private. The catering officer then found himself on the wrong end of a hefty rocket, threatened with the loss of his job, instructed to sort out the failings in the cookhouse, to go to the Paris food markets and use some imagination. The food improved dramatically.

Flt. Sgt. Collyer of the RAF police, a large, quietly-spoken, gentle man was a most unlikely occupant of his trade or rank. Ever anxious to salute, he even sat at his desk with the door open and hat on, ready to leap to his feet and salute any passing officer or, incredibly, one on the other end of his telephone! He lived locally with his French wife, and Sir Basil often summoned him to ask his advice on local matters. It is difficult to believe now that I, a humble SAC, had the temerity to goad such an outwardly imposing figure while he waited in our outer office to talk to Sir Basil: "Come on, Chiefy, have a seat and take the weight off your feet. Why don't you take your hat off while you wait?" He did, and proved to be nearly bald.

AC1 'Firmy' Laporte was a frightened little Frenchman of uncertain RAF trade who had exercised the little-known right available to citizens of NATO countries to undertake their National Service in the forces of a fellow member -country. We were rationed to 300 English cigarettes a week each, obtainable from the NAAFI at 50 francs (one shilling: 5p.) for twenty. Each Friday evening, 'Firmy', a Parisian, drove to Paris with his car (yes, he owned a CAR!) stuffed with non-smokers' fags sold to him at a small profit and destined for the black market. As far as I know he was never caught, though an RAF SP involved in the same trade was apprehended.

We were well served for entertainment at Camp Guynemer. The NAAFI provided an all-ranks cafeteria, a cinema showing English-language films, a snooker room and other amenities. There were weekly bingo sessions, with top prizes of sports cars and motor-cycles, and sometimes live entertainment. A top American singer of the day, Al Martino, performed once, and a highlight, the appearance of Ted Heath and his Band, sent British morale sky-high!

My time at AAFCE ended on a sad note. Some Wednesday afternoons I played in the HQ soccer team, run by Sgt. Fenny, as did 42-year old Wt. Off. Bert Moylan, a kind and gentle friend to all, who worked in HQ Intelligence Directorate. Luckily I was not in the team on my last Wednesday in

France, 27 October 1954. My friend and room-mate SAC David Mollart-Rogerson was keeping goal as usual when Wt. Off. Moylan, at right back, turned to speak to him, collapsed and died. Leaving the mess after tea next day, I was told by the 'Mekon', our bespectacled and vertically-challenged Corporal mess orderly, that I would be a member of the funeral party as I was of the right height. It was always nice to be able to disillusion an NCO somewhat full of his own importance, even if the occasion was a sad one.

All personnel other than those in the UK or Germany had to travel to RAF Innsworth for demobilisation, and that is where I finished my RAF service. Although I didn't appreciate it at the time, I had just completed two of the best years of my life. And what was Sir Basil Embry's impression of me? When I took my leave of him, still calling me Clayton, he described me as " ....a typical example of a young National Serviceman who came into the Service, did his bit to the best of his ability and returned from whence he had come as soon as he was able." Could have been worse!

❑ The author (2582282)

Having moved home many times as a child during the War, joining the RAF did not seem particularly strange. I underwent a medical and educational examination at Tavistock House in London in the autumn of 1952 and soon after my eighteenth birthday found myself, with several other conscripts, on a train to Warrington on 26 January 1953, bound for RAF Padgate. My memories of that place are sparse, but I do recall that the food was nowhere near the standards of home cooking, particularly the porridge! Kitting-out went well enough, and we learnt how to 'bull' the caps of our new boots by using a combination of Cherry Blossom polish, spit, and a red-hot spoon. As far as I know, I was in one of the first intakes to be issued with peaked caps as well as berets.

Then by train to 10 School of Recruit Training at RAF Melksham, a camp better known for technical training. There we were 'looked after' by Sgt. Robinson and Cpl. Wilson, dedicated sadists both, who put us spotty youths through the usual daily round of drill, PT, assault course, lectures, jabs and other strenuous activities. The weather didn't help, as it was very cold, snowy and generally unpleasant, but before long we began to feel the benefit of the training meted out by the DIs, who turned out to be quite human after all, under their gruff exteriors. At the end of the first three weeks or so at Melksham we were granted a 48-hour pass, and I travelled on one of the many coaches laid on to take us to London on our several ways home.

As soon as we returned, we were told that on 1 April 1953 there was to be a large parade in Manchester to mark the 35th birthday of the Royal Air Force, and some of us would be selected to take part. We then became the objects of much scrutiny by officers, SNCOs and anybody else who was passing, and I believe most of us genuinely wanted to be picked. And so I was, with about half the Flight. We then packed our kit, climbed aboard a fleet of RAF trucks and began the long trek northward to RAF Wilmslow, just outside Manchester, where our final training was to take place. What pleased us about that camp was the fact that WRAF girls were trained there, but little did we know that the chance of fraternising would be almost (but not quite!) nil. Our DIs accompanied us, and for the next four weeks we concentrated on drill, reaching the point where hundreds of airmen were drilling together, with the Central Band of the RAF and a number of regional bands, plus an RAF Regiment contingent. Soon the big day arrived, and we were inspected, white webbing belts and rifle slings at the ready, before being bussed in to the city. The large parade took place in Birchfields Park and was inspected by Field Marshall the Rt. Hon. Alexander of Tunis as aircraft, including the prototype Vulcan bomber, flew overhead. Then the whole parade marched, bayonets fixed, through the city to the strains of such music as 'Imperial Echoes" —a day to remember. This parade took the place of a normal passing-out parade, and next morning we received our postings before going on 14 days leave.

My job was to be an operations clerk, working in the control tower at RAF Moreton-in-Marsh in Gloucestershire. I reported there on 17 April and found my bedspace in hut 87A, a wooden hut with the usual coke stove in the middle. The work, for which there was 'on-the-job' training, was interesting, and comprised logging the movements of aircraft, using a simple switchboard, operating the VHF radio and driving the section's Land Rover on such tasks as towing the runway control caravan to its appointed position. When I arrived, the section was greatly over-manned, but as time went by people were 'demobbed' and not replaced, thus making greater demands on those left. I managed to achieve promotion through AC1 to LAC, SAC, and finally to Corporal (acting, paid) for the last six months of my service.

Living conditions at Moreton-in-Marsh were good. The food there was the best I had in the RAF, but at RAF Hospital Wroughton, where I was taken

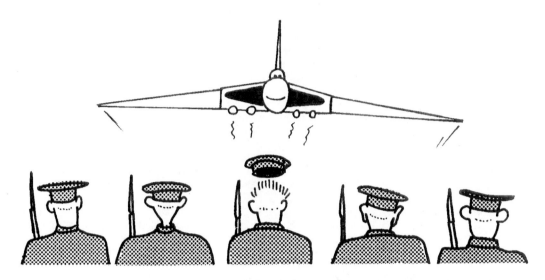

as an out-patient after dropping the towbar of the runway caravan on my foot, it was the worst — almost uneatable!

My friends and I managed to go home quite often, as there was only flying at weekends if the weather had been bad enough to hold up the course programme, Moreton being the home of a flying training school. Most Thursday evenings (Thursday being pay-day) were spent in the White Hart hotel in the village, where the drink of the time was the 'Tom Collins', a gin concoction guaranteed to make the mile-and-a-half trek to camp an unsteady one! On Saturdays when I didn't go home, having found a girl friend in the village, there was the chance of a trip to Cheltenham Town Hall to a dance at which such bands as Sid Phillips' or Eric Delaney's would be playing.

After a home trip, I and several of my fellow-residents of the hut used to arrive at Moreton on the train from London which got in at about 00.30 on Monday mornings. We then walked to camp, and turned on Radio Luxemburg to hear Jack Jackson's Record Round-up as soon as we reached the hut, waking up anyone already asleep in the process. It didn't pay to go to bed on a Sunday evening! Such is the thoughtlessness of youth!

On the whole, I enjoyed my two years in the RAF, apart from the usual frustrations of waiting for somebody to make his mind up, and upon 'demob' on 25 January 1955 I joined the Royal Auxiliary Air Force for voluntary service in the same trade. In fact, after a visit to RAF North Weald in December 1953, I had 'signed on' in the RAuxAF on 1 January, thus being in two services at the same time!

❑ Mr. Trevor Brown (2585050)

My period of service started on 3 March 1953, when I reported to the reception unit at RAF Padgate, where I also did my basic training. At the end of our 'square-bashing', most of my Flight were sent home on indefinite leave and told that our postings would be sent on to us. I was eventually posted to the RAF Records Office at Barnwood, Gloucester, on 27 May 1953 for on-the-job training as a Clerk (Org.). I duly arrived at the domestic site at RAF Innsworth and after the formalities reported to my office in the 'Glasshouse' at Barnwood. My first task was to complete a Form 295A for a special weekend grant to commemorate the Queen's coronation the following Tuesday, 2 June. Not a bad life, I thought, almost three weeks leave after 'square-bashing', three days at a new unit and then a four-day grant!

My first few months at Barnwood were spent working on Local Unit Establishments. I was then moved to a newly-created section — CID (Central Information Department) — in Air Staff Headquarters, providing graphs and other statistical information to the AOC, Air Commodore W. E. Richards.

One Friday morning towards the end of my two years, an article appeared in the Daily Mirror, written by Keith Waterhouse. It gave his view on how he had spent his two years National Service in the RAF as a clerk. He thought it had been a complete waste of time, and my colleagues and I agreed with a lot of what he had written. The article created quite a few ripples within the Headquarters, and Mr. Waterhouse's personal file was collected from the 'bin room' for perusal by Air Staff officers.

Like every other National Serviceman, I kept a demob. chart**, religiously crossing off on first entering the office every day. Eventually demob. day arrived and I was released to 'Civvie Street'. Looking back, the two years did me no harm; physically I have never been as fit as when I was doing my 'square-bashing'.

**Not everybody did! [Editor]

❏ Sqdn. Ldr. J. D. Stabler (2589790)

I was 18 years and 3 weeks old when I went to RAF Padgate for my uniform etc. On my trip to the barber's, I remember, I saw a Teddy Boy I'd seen on the platform at Euston and who was in my billet, waiting for his regulation haircut. He had rather long hair, and the barber said to him "Won't keep you long, lad, with that weight on your head". As the scissors were wielded the barber said "I've found his ears" and at the end of the cut he said "Now write home and tell your mother you're a boy!".

My recruit training was at RAF Hednesford, Staffordshire. Then I went to RAF Weeton, near Blackpool, for training as a Flying Clothing Worker (FCW) in Safety & Surface, Trade Group 13. When I left after the six-week course I had the rank of AC1. I was posted to RAF Chivenor in Devon and after six months I automatically received the rank of LAC. There I remained for the rest of my service. As a result of my efforts I eventually reached the rank of SAC and left with that rank. I had attained the necessary education standard to be promoted to Corporal but it was very apparent that as I wasn't prepared to sign on for a further year I wasn't going to get it.

I thoroughly enjoyed my time in the Service and joined the Air Training Corps as an instructor, eventually being commissioned in the RAFVR (T).

❏ Mr. Vernon Place (2712368)

I joined the RAF in November 1953 and remember going by train from Cambridge to RAF Cardington for kitting out ready for square-bashing. At Cardington, the thing that sticks in my mind was the great big hangars, and having a haircut. One Welsh boy had a lot of bright ginger hair which they cropped off completely, making him look like a shorn sheep!

Having kitted out, we were herded onto a train and went to RAF Padgate, where we did our 'square-

bashing'. At that time of year it was extremely cold and damp. Because I'd played in a brass band at home in Cambridgeshire I joined the voluntary band when I got to Padgate, and then played on every passing-out parade from the first week I was there, having marched only in village bands before! Once it was so cold that our instruments froze up, leaving only the drums to provide music. There was a very fat Corporal who played the bass drum. One day when the parade ground was very icy he was playing merrily away when he slipped and did a slow roll over the top of his drum, much to our delight, Corporals during basic training not being our favourite people! The NCO in charge of our hut, Cpl. Race, was an ex-Guardsman, and everything about him was just a little bit different from everyone else. He used to mix a bit of white with the blue applied to his webbing, to make them a little lighter in colour. His rifle sling was loose so that every time he 'presented arms' it made a lovely noise against the rifle. A very strict man, but we came to like him eventually. He found out that I used to put my trousers under the mattress every night to make creases and he then told me to do the same for him, and God help me if I didn't do it properly and created 'tram-line' creases! Because I did that I didn't have to do other duties around the hut.

After 'square-bashing' I went to RAF Melksham for trade training. My hut number was 28, the band hut, in which there were both sprogs like me and experienced men, so I learnt a lot about life in the RAF. Some of them got up to all sorts of tricks. Sometimes you would come back to find your bed up in the rafters, for example. I was to be an electrical mechanic/ground, but as I had worked on the land for my father, a smallholder, I found studying difficult at first. In the end, however, I survived and in fact gained a certificate for 'outstanding ability', which my mother promptly put up on the wall. I recently found some of my study books and I'm quite amazed how much I learnt.

We were allowed to keep motor-cycles on camp provided we had crash helmets, and could leave camp on trips instead of taking part in sports afternoons, and so were able to visit such places as Cheddar Gorge, which we would probably not have seen otherwise. The six months were very hard-working and very useful. Having passed out successfully, I was posted to RAF Stoke Heath in Shropshire, a Maintenance Unit adjoining RAF Ternhill.

At Stoke Heath, the work sites were up to three miles from the living quarters, which were called Longford Camp, so we were all issued with bicycles. I found myself having to remember three numbers — my service number, my bicycle number, and my cornet number (because I joined the band at Stoke Heath). Life there was completely different to anything else I'd experienced in the RAF. Because of my training, my job was electroplating, in what was probably the only plating shop in the RAF at the time. We did chrome, copper, cadmium and silver plating, and most of my time was spent on silver-plating; many of the items I handled were not RAF pieces. We worked on a radar site, so there was a very strict guard there. On one occasion we took a bumper bar in to the plating shop by marching in close order with the bumper between us, as our Flight Sergeant had told us that if we had the initiative to get it in to the shop, he would get it out. Later on, an SP asked me how we got it out, as he'd seen it go in and was waiting to charge us with one or more offences when he saw it going out, but he never did! We often worked on plating metal pieces before an AOC's inspection, and so were generally in the good books of those in authority. We chromium-plated all the shiny parts of the Queen's Land Rover, quite a painstaking task, and also I silvered the underside of Montgomery's wash-basin! One lad was stripping old chrome off a bumper bar in an acid bath and was covered in acid in an explosion.

The band at Stoke Heath was quite large, and there was also a pipe band and drums, so we could go to places to play at large functions. On one occasion we were flown to Andover in two Dakotas to play for a combined services parade. If it was necessary to augment other bands we went to help, so we visited several other places — better than sitting about doing nothing. Another enjoyable thing was visiting Jack's Café near the camp, to have mugs of hot tea and bacon sandwiches dripping with fat.

At Longford Camp the boiler house was near our hut, and in the winter after work we used to 'acquire' a shovelful of red-hot coke to get our hut stove started. Before long the inmates of other huts caught on to this idea, to the detriment of the central hot water system, and it wasn't long before hot water was in short supply. Eventually the boiler house was put off limits.

In the summer before I was demobbed I was put on a charge — Misuse of RAF Property. I've mentioned that we cycled backwards and forwards between camp and work site. On a very hot day we wouldn't go right back to our hut to get mugs in which to have a cold drink, so we used to have soup plates filled with lemonade and drink it with a spoon. A Flight Sergeant who had been in the RAF for a very long time and who seemed to have a grudge against us charged the whole lot of us. We

didn't know what the charge was going to be called until we were marched in, left-right, left-right. The charge was dismissed, but I was told not to do it again! A very silly thing, and although it was not the reason I didn't sign on it would have contributed to my decision.

There was a group of about seven of us who used to pay £1 each to be brought in the direction of home in an old estate car belonging to one of us who lived (and still does) in Newmarket, close to my home. Once as we came up over the brow of a hill the half-shaft broke and a wheel overtook us! There was a smell of smoke, and the car emptied very quickly! That group of men had a reunion in 1989, prior to which I'd visited our old camp to take photos. My old hut is now used for storing antiques. The floor is not quite so well polished nowadays! Surprisingly, all seven of us are still with the same partners we had then. Jack's Café is still there, but is for sale as it has been replaced by a newer building.

As a young lad from a Fenland village I was given a wonderful opportunity to meet people from other walks of life and my service had a great effect on shaping my future life. I found great friendship with many people, although a few others I didn't mind never seeing again. Lots of people regretted going into the RAF for National Service, but looking back I see it as an eventful time in my life and I certainly don't regret it. I want to pay a tribute to one organisation which was very important to us, particularly during basic and trade training, and that's the Salvation Army. We used to go to the SA Club, where we were given a great welcome and made to feel 'at home'.

❏ Mr. D. M. Cook (3142331)

Prior to 1953 I was a Post Office Telephones apprentice and had no desire to go to the Korean War with the Royal Signals, the regiment most Telephone staff joined, as I had spent a number of years in the Air Training Corps, included in which was a cadet radio course at RAF Halton. Most of us cadets applied for an aircrew test, which was done at RAF Hornchurch, and I have a feeling that I went there twice, possibly once as a cadet and once just before National Service.

By December 1953, I didn't think that I would be sent for until early in 1954, but a rail warrant arrived for RAF Cardington, where we were kitted out for a week before being bussed in the fog to RAF Hednesford for 'square-bashing' just before Christmas 1953. I recall us Scots being on camp doing fire picket duty over Christmas and New Year period, compensated by the fact that we had two

Christmas dinners, the official one and the one on Christmas Day. The benefits of ATC training made these early weeks easier for ex-cadets. I recall coffee stall caravans at the Hednesford camp gate selling hot dogs late at night, and also I remember Saturday night dances at local villages.

From Hednesford the next stop was Radio School at RAF Compton Bassett in Wiltshire, where I think we were to be trained as wireless mechanics, but as the class was made up of ex-Post Office telephone apprentices, of whom many had been ATC cadets and most of us held City & Guilds Telecommunications Certificates, the powers that be put us on the Inter-Command Transmitter Fitters course. We all thought this was good due to the equipment implying an overseas posting. Most of the summer of 1954 was taken up by trade study with RAF and civilian instructors.

Chippenham NAAFI Club had just been opened, and I remember going there a lot. Most of the Scots lads were into ballroom dancing, and I remember having a regular partner at dances there and at the Ecko Radio factory at Melksham, and in Swindon there was a band that played Victor Silvester-type music. The journey from Calne to Chippenham was often on the 'Calne Flyer', a couple of railway carriages old enough to have gas lighting.

Walls' had a sausage factory in Calne, and pig-swill vans collected from the RAF camp. We used to joke about the food cycle: RAF cookhouse to pigs to sausages to RAF cookhouse!

The local drink seemed to be halves of cider and Guinness, and I recall a few of us walking back to Compton Bassett arguing the merits of Humphrey Littleton's "Bad Penny Blues". You may remember the trad. jazz versus modern jazz furore of the time. Seems strange now that such things got feelings so worked up. "The Goon Show" seemed popular, with the billets full of chaps listening to the broadcast over the Tannoy. There didn't seem to be much in the way of personal belongings; one or two chaps had Agfa cameras and used the camp camera club darkroom.

Came the end of the course, and I remember one admin. type saying "You're lucky, you've got RAF Anstruther!", to which I replied "Where's that?" and was told that it was in Fife, Scotland, on the north side of the River Forth. In the 1950s, before the Forth and Tay road bridges were built, it meant using bus and ferry-boat or the infrequent coastal train. Close to Dundee it may have been, but it was awkward to reach on a Sunday.

RAF Anstruther was a Ground Control Interception (GCI) Station with a buried control site, height-finding radar site, R/T transmitter site and receiver site and some miles away down in Anstruther village on the coast a domestic site, all relatively modern. Years later the domestic site was made into a holiday camp, with the guardroom as a site office or shop. Shifts were changed by using a bus which toured the sites. The RAF dogs which roamed the aerial sites were really scary; guard them they certainly did!

After training on HF transmitters, a bit of work had to be done to learn the VHF transmitter, helped by doing some mods to narrow the band width to suit the Hunter fighters that had come into service at RAF Leuchars. These used to go out in pairs to do practice interceptions (PIs), one hunting the other. In the summer months we had WRAF part-time radar operators come up for their annual camp. The radar operators used to have a joke about the trainees mixing up a target with a permanent echo, a favourite being the Bass Rock, which sits in the River Forth, and there was much humour about how many Hunters had shot it down. The USAF used to fly B-47 Stratojets over the control area and there were UHF sets for speaking to them, and Neptunes used to visit Leuchars from Kinloss or Lossiemouth.

During some exercises we used Ferrograph tape recorders to broadcast aero-engine noise to jam things and we were quick to see how tape recorders would become popular. Those of us with portable record players used to arrange some sort of dancing in the NAAFI for the visiting WRAF annual campers.

At Anstruther it was pointed out that as it was a small camp it was not possible to provide much in the way of welfare, but such money as there was went to help the mess budget. There were few complaints about the food — we ate well.

At that time, National Servicemen could sign on for a further year, but this didn't fit in with the Post Office Telephones training programme. We did meet the odd chap who was studying for university who found the RAF encouragement to study worth the extra year, and since they were paid as regulars they could save for further studies.

All the sporting types really seemed to enjoy the service facilities and competitions. The nearest I got to sport was when my mother decided to knit a big polo-necked sweater for her son in the RAF. One could go for Sunday breakfast in a polo-neck. Mine was bright red, and my wearing it to a breakfast stimulated interest from a chap who was a goalkeeper in one of the camp football teams.

We went into the RAF on a wage of 28 shillings (£1.40) per week and after home allotment deductions a crisp 10-shilling note was handed out at pay parade. One thing quickly learned about National Service was the value of mother and money. Trying to be a Romeo on ten bob a week less haircuts etc. really sharpened the wits! I always felt lucky that I didn't get into a shooting war and am eternally grateful to the guys who did so on our behalf.

❑ Mr. Derek Turnidge (2591546)

After enrolment at RAF Cardington on 14 September 1954 I did my basic training at RAF Hednesford. On 29 November I was posted to RAF Shawbury to join the first specialist course for Operations Clerks, who had previously been trained 'on the job'. My final posting was to RAF Wattisham in Suffolk on 4 January 1955, and there I remained until the end of my service in September 1956, apart from a two-week detachment to Washington Hall in the summer of that year to learn how to put out fires if nuclear war happened.

Block 59, Room 4 at Wattisham was very unusual in having a telephone (ext. 222) on the Station netweork. That phone played a part in two episodes, the first of which was more a rite of passage. Wattisham was equipped with a CR/DF (cathode ray direction finder) and so was available to provide bearings on aircraft transmissions. This was particularly helpful in the case of aircraft in distress, and bearings from two or more locations would enable an accurate fix to be obtained on the aircraft in trouble. Whenever, therefore, no flying was taking place, the control tower would be manned by one operations clerk solely for the purpose of providing bearings on the International Distress frequency, 121.5 mHz. The custom was for someone in the billet to 'phone the tower when an ops. clerk was doing his first night duty alone, assume an American accent and claim to be a controller at nearby USAF Bentwaters. The story would be that they had an emergency and needed to divert a number of aircraft to Wattisham at once. Until the unfortunate airman tumbled to the fact that he was being taken for a ride, it naturally caused a great deal of mirth for everyone listeining in the comfort of the billet!

The second episode was potentially more serious. At that time, one of the two Hunter squadrons at Wattisham — 257 and 263 — was regularly involved in Operation Fabulous, which involved aircraft being armed and at a high state of readiness from a little before dawn to a little after dusk. We were so indoctrinated with the need for secrecy that among ourselves we always referred to the 'Unmentionable' rather than the word Fabulous.

On this particular occasion our watch was to be on duty in the tower before dawn. My duties included driving the Land Rover, and because of problems with the remote controlled switching arrangements for the airfield lights I had been instructed on how to put on the necessary lights by driving to two sub-stations on the airfield to turn on the lights from there. I therefore booked an early call from the guardroom and duly went to sleep with a towel draped over the foot of my bed so that I could easily be identified in the dark. I was woken, signed the 'chitty' thrust before me, looked at my watch and realised that I had been called thirty minutes early. Knowing that the rest of the watch would not take kindly to being woken yet, I decided to sit up and wait a little longer. The next thing I remember was the 'phone ringing to find out where the duty ops. clerks were!

I doubt if I have ever moved so fast since. I woke up the rest of the watch, rushed off to the MT section to get the Land Rover, drove round the airfield at high speed to turn on the lights and then went to the tower to face the music. Fortunately the controller on duty was amenable to my apology and nothing more became of the matter and the safety of the country was presumably not prejudiced!

❑ Sqdn. Ldr. Peter W. Davies (2738248)

I joined the Air Ministry Met. Office in November 1953 as a civilian Scientific Assistant at RAF Wittering, so when I was called up for National Service I had already served for six months in that post. There was a clause in the 1948 National Service Act which stated that anyone with that qualification could elect to do their National Service as an airman meteorologist. I so elected, and my Airman's Service Book shows me attested at the rank of AC2 on 28 October 1954 and promoted to the rank of SAC on the very same day! Thus I was an SAC even before departing from RAF Cardington for basic training at RAF Hednesford. There were a number of airman Met. Assistants on the intake, and we only put up our three-bladed prop badges on completion of 'square-bashing'; nevertheless, two months' SAC back-pay was a nice Christmas present!

Hednesford was dictated by the fact that I was a holder of a number of the then 'O'-levels and was classified as POM (Potential Officer Material), almost all of whom went to Hednesford at that time. Most of one week during basic training was set aside for trade assessment. As my trade was already decided, I was at a loose end, a very dangerous

STAND BY YER BEDS!

'Bull' night.

Getting a body fit...

Below: A squad of recruits lined up at 3SoRT, Padgate, apparently ready for a session of PT, clutching their towels and kit.

Right: Recruits and staff pose for the camera at 7SoRT, Bridgnorth.

Rifle drill at RAF Bridgnorth in the late 1950s, the recruits wearing and unusual combination of peaked cap and battle-dress uniform. (Mr D, Miller)

Right: These three Drill Instructors at 3 SoRT, Padgate were typical of their trade - smart and keen to turn out efficient recruits. The one on the left, Cpl XXXXXXXXXXXX added some Blanco to his Air Force Blue webbing cleaner to give it a more distinctive colour! (Mr M. Place)

A passing-out parade at 3SoRT, Padgate, with a number of proud parents seated on the left. (Mr V. Place)

condition during 'square-bashing', and I became extremely familiar with the insides of the three cookhouses! Most afternoons that week were spent lugging Bren guns and ammunition from the armoury to the ranges and back. One slight benefit was that one took the NAAFI break (i.e. a fag and a pint of revolting tea) with the staff instructors in the dry instead of with the recruits in rain and/or snow!

After basic training, I went to 11 Group, Fighter Command, and from January 1955 served at RAF Wattisham (with detachments to North Weald, Oakington, Waterbeach, West Malling and Stradishall); and RAF Waterbeach from May 1955 The last eighteen months or so of my service were spent at El Adem in Libya, with detachments all over the Middle East. The UK Government was, at the time, giving technical assistance to the new Government of King Idris (well before Ghadaffi appeared on the scene) in setting up a Libyan National Met. Service, thus I went on detachments to the Libyan offices in Cyrenaica and elsewhere. Being a Met. Assistant I supposedly knew the top of a plotting chart from the bottom, which appeared to be sufficient qualification for me to become 2nd. navigator on the RAF El Adem Desert Rescue Service! Many happy hours were spent in the middle of the Sahara Desert digging Austin 30-cwt. trucks out of soft sand! Also, supposedly knowing about the weather, I was frequently called upon to be supernumary aircrew observer in Shackletons flying recce sorties all over the Med. and the Sahara. In reality, I spent much of that time as Chief Galley Slave — you try producing meals in a 'Shack'!

The crowning glory of my National Service was becoming a Corporal (temporary, acting, local, unpaid), complete with chalk stripes on my hairy blue battledress jacket, for three days in charge of a gang of six other NS airmen at the bombing range forty-odd miles from El Adem during its calibration!

After demobilisation at RAF Innsworth in October 1956, I returned as a civilian to the Met. Office at RAF Wittering. In 1973 I was commissioned into the RAF Reserve of Officers, using my original service number.

☐ Mr. F. W. King (2740706)

I served from November 1954 to November 1956, during which time I went to RAF Cardington for kitting-out, RAF Hednesford ('square-bashing'), RAF Melksham (12 SoTT) and finally 32 MU at RAF St. Athan. From there, about a month before being 'demobbed', I went on a two-week fire-fighting course at Washington Hall, Chorley, Lancashire, which at that time was normal procedure for RAF personnel about to leave the service. It was also a kind of reunion, as many of us who had started our service together finally met up.

My introduction to the RAF was when I arrived at Bedford by train, was shunted onto a bus and deposited at RAF Cardington on a sunny afternoon, noticing as I arrived the huge airship hangars which are a landmark there. After four or five days, on account of 'them' having lost my paperwork, I was unable to proceed to my 'square-bashing' camp, and was placed in the so-called Transit hut, and I stayed on the Station for about three weeks. With me was a chap who had already done a year of his service before being released on compassionate grounds to help his parents on their smallholding. He had now returned to do his final bit as a service policeman — a nice chap. The pair of us managed to get a weekend pass, as the authorities probably felt sorry for us.

While at Cardington I was one of several men subjected to a form of medical test which involved three jabs in my palm side of my right wrist, something to do with TB, I think. Unfortunately, the first three jabs didn't come up to expectations, so I had another three in my left wrist for luck, and these proved OK. One had the feeling of being used as a guinea pig.

We arrived at RAF Hednesford on a Friday afternoon after the journey by bus with our packed lunches. After being billeted (mine was Hut 74, D Sqdn., 14 Flight, 1 Wing), we were given our 'jabs' — nobody slept that night, and next morning we were on the square trying to lift our arms up and down while being shouted at from all angles by the DIs. January and February were at times rather cold and snowy months, and shaving and washing in cold water did a lot for one's complexion! I well remember trying to dress after PT, with frozen fingers — what a nightmare. We all remember what we had to keep our huts warm with — large round black stoves. I dread to think of the number of tins of polish we used to start it up, but how red the top glowed once we did! And the bind of 'bull night' cleaning it up.

RAF Hednesford produced a few tales, including the time when live .303 ammunition was accidentally thrown on a fire which was used to burn the cardboard packing in which the bullets came. The bullet went through the nearest DI's upper lip, but he survived. This was the nearest I got to unarmed combat.

Now on to RAF Melksham, close to a lovely little town with the River Avon running through it. It

53

was while I was stationed there that I got married. Because of camp close-down during Whitsun, my wife and I thought it was an opportunity not to be missed. Father-in-law was not very happy at the time due to the short notice. Also while I was at Melksham, I became rather poorly, and once home on the Saturday afternoon the family doctor was called and diagnosed tonsilitis. Within an hour, I was on the way to an army hospital at Sherford Camp in an ambulance, but was home again on the following Thursday.

After trade training as an instrument mechanic, I was posted to RAF St. Athan in South Wales (the nearest I got to going abroad), quite close to my home at Taunton in Somerset. On a Saturday I would be home by 15.45 after catching a bus to Cardiff and a train from there to Taunton, using my 1250 to get the reduced fare of 11/3 (56p.). When I first arrived at St. Athan, I was allocated a bedspace in a room in a three-storey block; there were six rooms to a block and 22 airmen in each room. Goodbye to black stoves — these blocks were centrally heated and had bedside lights. I was advised by another airman to 'skive off' for the weekend, as being the middle of Friday afternoon it was not worth signing in and nobody knew I had arrived. So I took a chance and went home, where I worried all the weekend, but when I arrived back on Sunday evening the Corporal in charge was not around, so come Monday morning I carried on as usual with the normal signing-in process.

From the window of my room on the third floor, I could see a field in which for a long time stood two Wellington bombers. One dinner-time, after returning my mug (which I still have) and irons to my bedside locker, I looked out of the window and saw a huge fire where the Wellingtons had stood. What a sorry sight, so sad and short-sighted.

One Saturday morning (remember we only had one Saturday morning off per month unless we had done something special like giving blood or being on a Guard of Honour — yes, I've even done that), a gang of us had to move a dozen card tables from a C of E church to an RC church and the only transport we had was, you might have guessed, a Queen Mary!

Wednesday afternoon was sports afternoon, and one was always expected to participate in one sport or another, no matter what the weather. My forte was a trot down to the beach at Boverton, until one very stormy afternoon. Whilst we waited for the storm to pass over, the section WO visited our billet and found many of us not in sports gear. Fortunately, those like me at the far end of the billet were ready to go by the time the WO reached us, but too late, we

were booked and put on a 252. We got away with it, but the card players didn't!

I entered the RAF not wanting to leave a well-paid job to come down to a pay of a few shillings a week, and to leave my home was a bit of a wrench, but having served my time I was glad not to have missed it. The value of comradeship it gave and the outlook on life that I never had before was invaluable, something that is missing today. I still have in my possession 65 items of paperwork from which my history for those two years can easily be traced. The items include all ten of my Pay Account sheets (RAF Form 4074); temporary passes Form 295; posting instructions from RAF Hednesford; inoculation and vaccination certificates; permanent passes from RAF Melksham and RAF St. Athan; photos of how bedding and kit inspections should be laid out; a booklet showing improvements in pay and bounties dated 20 February 1956; and a Statement of Service and Certificate on Discharge, RAF Form 1394.

❏ Mr. Mike Minson (5028932)

At eighteen and a half years of age, I was inducted into the RAF on 23 August 1956. Having been bombed out of East London during the war, I had lived a fairly sheltered life at Barnehurst in suburban Kent, and National Service proved to be a cultural, psychological and sometimes physical shock! I well remember waiting on the platform at Marylebone Station for the train to RAF Cardington, where it would all begin. Others on the platform were clearly in the same boat — they all looked dead worried! Arrival at Cardington was a bit of an anti-climax — no shouting DIs or overt discipline. We stayed there a few days, gradually adding to our kit and wandering round in hybrid get-ups as a result. I think that it was at this stage that we saw the VD and anti-smoking films, both graphic American productions and enough to put you off sex and smoking for life! There was a general air of unreality among the conscripts, soon, however, to be brutally dissipated by the dreadful shock of 'square-bashing' camp.

After about a week at Cardington we embarked on a special train, destination RAF Padgate. We found out later that Padgate was slowly sinking into a marsh and it was closed soon after we left. We were met at Warrington station and taken in three-tonners to the camp. For some reason we couldn't quite fathom, the lorries drove onto a grassed area. Climbing down, we were suddenly confronted by four DIs, complete with slashed peak caps, looking like the Gestapo and appearing to be on the verge of iapoplexy because we had disembarked onto the grass! The fact that even Jesse Owens couldn't have jumped to the nearest tarmac didn't seem to impress them. Looking back, this was clearly an intimidatory introduction specifically (and perhaps necesssarily) designed to terrify and inculcate in us a healthy fear of these individuals, who suddenly appeared to have the power of life and death over us. I suppose I was realistic enough in a dim sort of way to appreciate why it was being done, but I remember as time went by becoming increasingly resentful of the four in question, who we quickly realised didn't have the IQ of a rabbit between them! And so life began at Stalag Luft Padgate! Discipline was extremely strict and there were endless 'bull' sessions on personal and communal equipment. The floor of the hut was of polished lino, and it was strictly forbidden to walk on it; one had to remove one's boots at the door and skate down the room on blanket pads so as to avoid any possibility of a mark. Everyone was desperately homesick and scared witless of what the morrow might bring, but again looking back, they gradually began to make service personnel out of us. It was clearly unthinkable to try to buck the system and nobody did. However, on a very sombre note, there were two suicides during our our eight-week stay, both dreadful hangings, but neither in our Flight, I'm glad to say. During the eight weeks, only one 36-hour pass was allowed. By

the time I arrived home it was very nearly time to go back, and the heartbreakingly few hours in the bosom of my family was unreal and spent in trepidation of my return. I recall being let out of camp on a couple of Saturdays and have a memory of watching football at Old Trafford.

Back at the ranch our life of purgatory went on. There were endless drills, 'bull' sessions, kit inspections and rising at the crack of dawn. The word was that there was bromide in the tea, although it never seemed to affect my libido — not that it was ever put to the test! The food was pretty ghastly too, but we ate it; the alternative was to starve. On one memorable drill session the lead marchers turned left over a shouted order of "turn right" and ended up facing a blank wall! Up raced a particularly nasty DI, eyeballed them closely and shouted into their faces "You ****bags, you ballsed it up". At that moment a gust of wind blew the DI's hat off, revealing a skull so closely shaven as to look like a billiard ball. This was too much: despite our inherent fear, many simply burst out laughing, and to our enormous surprise the DI joined in. Five minutes later he was exhorting us to "Swing them arms or I'll tear them off and hit you with the soggy end"!

"Swing them arms or I'll tear them off and hit you with the soggy end"!

The eight weeks, which seemed like eight years, finally drew to a close. At that time there was only one place in the world where the British forces were on active service — Cyprus. I simply knew I would finish up there, but prayed continually that I wouldn't. But to no avail: when the postings came through there was AC2 Minson, destined for HQ Middle East Air Force, Nicosia. There followed the ordeal of 'jabs'. Battle-hardened veterans (as they now saw themselves) were dropping like flies as they approached the doctor, before they had the jabs, and many others dropped afterwards. They were a bit grim; I felt pretty queasy for a few hours and thereafter supported a large itchy scab, affectionately referred to by the lads as a cat's *****!

However, first there was to be trade training. With my Civil Service background I was selected to be a Clerk/Organisation and sent to RAF Credenhill, near Hereford, for six weeks. By this time winter was upon us, and my principal memory of Credenhill is returning from 36-hour passes at 02.00 hours on the Monday mornings to a literally freezing barracks, and in the knowledge of an 06.00 reveille! My train fare home was 28/6 (£1.425), 2/6 (12.5p) more than my weekly pay. But after Padgate, Credenhill was a doddle. Discipline was much more relaxed, and I actually began to believe I was a human being again. The training was quite comprehensive, and among other matters I got up to 35 w.p.m. on the typewriter. One weekend I looked up a girl I knew in Pontypridd — female company after the long weeks of enforced celibacy I had endured was a tonic!

Then on to Gloucester for embarkation preparation, including the issue of tropical kit. I was to be spared the sea journey, which I later heard was horrendous, and flew on a chartered DC-6 out of Southend. As no overflying of European countries while we were in uniform was permitted we had to go the long way round over the Bay of Biscay, refuelling at Malta and then on up the Med., in a total flying time of ten hours. We arrived at HQ MEAF in mid-January 1957. The camp site was arid and depressing and the facilities (deep trench latrines etc.) primitive, but the good news was that a move to Episkopi on the coast was imminent. We duly moved there lock, stock and barrel and heard later that one of the lorries had been blown off the road by a EOKA mine.

Episkopi was a pleasant surprise - a vast camp with good sports and social facilities and with new barrack blocks nearing completion. I spent the first six months in a four-man marquee-type tent. One of my compatriots was an official driver, a mad Welshman who kept trying to beat the Episkopi to Nicosia record by car. The roads were poorly surfaced, precipitous and seldom straight and Harry drove like a madman. I still can't understand why he didn't kill himself; the fact that he was a brilliant driver probably counted. One or two of his less talented colleagues were killed or badly injured, and it was a constant source of concern to the 'powers that be'. Even worse, he prevailed upon me to break the serviceman's golden rule - Never Volunteer. In my spare time I used to draw a S&W .38 revolver and go with him as escort to some officer or other. Usually I had a few drinks in Nicosia to anaesthetise myself for the jorney home. I didn't quite do a Pope John when I got out of the car, but it was a near thing!

Our tent lines used deep trench latrines and it was not long before I and a good few others caught a nasty case of amoebic dysentry. This meant a three-week stay in the nearby Akrotiri Military Hospital. After a week I had more or less recovered, and it was wonderful being looked after by the nurses, although they all seemed to be officers and therefore beyond the reach of erks such as us.

I found myself working in the Establishments Section, which was responsible for manning and equipment over a vast area spanning Malta, north and east Africa and the Persian Gulf. It was interesting work made even more tolerable by the management style of the officers i/c, a Wg. Cdr. and a Sqdn. Ldr. (both pilots), who were officers and gentlemen in every sense of the word. They did everything in their power to make life easier for their staff and were on hand when one ran into problems. The working hours were 07.00 to 13.00 throughout the year, but the resultant free time was heavily eroded by guard duties. EOKA waxed and waned, and fortunately for us they lacked any real explosive experts. While I was on guard duty at the armoury one night, a bomb went off at 02.00 in the nearby empty cinema and everyone came rushing out of the tent lines. At 19.00 the previous evening the cinema had been packed out, and if EOKA had got the timing right there could have been a massacre. On another occasion while coming off main road guard duty with a friend, his Sten gun strap broke and the gun dropped butt-first onto the ground. He had left the magazine on, and the whole lot went off! I'll never forget standing there frozen while the bloody thing jumped about scattering rounds, but fortunately nobody was hurt. At John's Court Martial we heard that it was alleged that when the weapon was retrieved the safety-catch was found to be 'on'! There had been other incidents with this notoriously inaccurate, unreliable, old and worn out weapon, and this was the last straw. A number of us, including myself, wrote to our MPs complaining about dangerous weapons and the food. To its great credit the RAF acted swiftly to rectify the situation. Within a few weeks we were issued with new Sterling guns and a new Warrant Officer cook (of Italian extraction as it happened) was appointed, transforming the mess generally and the food in particular.

By this time I was dating one of the WRAF girls on the section, a lovely girl from Dundee, one of whose voluntary duties was to baby-sit for the officers. Both officers lived with their families in nice, albeit prefabricated, houses, and it became a real pleasure to join my girl friend on these 'duties'. We were always left a sumptuous buffet and rarely saw the kids. The Officers' Club at HQ MEAF was luxurious, and our two officers and their wives liked to patronise it, hence the frequent baby-sitting.

An amusing, if risqué, event took place in the Sergeants' Mess, which was also quite luxurious. The NCOs were throwing a party and invited all the officers. A few erks like myself were also invited — we never ound out why, but it might have had something to do with our own Sergeant. As the riotous evening wore on, we could see a young Plt. Off. getting more and more smashed. Finally he staggered upright onto a table and at the top of his voice shouted out "Bring me a ****ing woman". There was an instant silence, akin to when the batwing doors swing open in a Western, and into it the CO, a Gp. Capt., said icily and penetratingly "Take that man to his room". We never saw that Plt. Off. again; rumour had it that he was given a 'disciplinary' posting to Sharjah, where the humidity is a stifling 98%, for 'conduct unbecoming an officer and gentleman'.

I was shortly in hot water myself. HQ MEAF also contained units of the Army and Navy, and one day when I was crossing the quadrangle I was stopped by an Army Warrant Officer who accused me of being improperly dressed. He was right: I had plain black civilian shoes on, virtually indistinguishable from the RAF ones, which were in for repair. He formally charged me, and in due course I was marched up in front of our own officers. The charge was read out while I stood rigidly to attention in considerable trepidation, for this was my first-ever charge. Then came another memorable moment. The Wg. Cdr. turned to the Sqdn. Ldr. and said firmly "I will not have my men being charged by these brown jobs - case dismissed". I was marched out in a daze and in the corridor the Flt. Sgt. hissed "You were lucky there, lad".

Shortly afterwards came the most memorable

incident of all and one which reinforced my high regard for our two officers. I was seeking to have seven weeks' leave back in Blighty, spanning Christmas and my birthday, and found to my dismay that I was in a Catch 22 situation. The EOKA problem had flared up again and we were forbidden to leave camp unless in uniform and armed. The civilian airlines at Nicosia, sixty miles away, would not accept uniformed personnel in any circumstances, so it appeared I was stuck. I decided to take my problem direct to the Wg. Cdr., who expressed sympathy and asked me to leave it with him. Two days later he came up with a cunning plan which worked perfectly. On the day of my scheduled departure I was to be appointed as his special messenger and was to report to the Episkopi guardroom, where I would be given 'secret documents' to take by hand to the CO at nearby Akrotiri air base. After the journey by jeep to Akrotiri I was to deliver the documents and then find my way to the airfield, where the C-in-C's flight would be waiting to take him to Nicosia. The Wg. Cdr. then stressed that the next bit was absolutely crucial to the cunning plan: I was to get into the very rear of the plane and play Brer Rabbit — lie low and say nuffin'. The C-in-C would embark and off we would go. At the military section of Nicosia airport he would disembark to review a guard of honour, and I would stay put while the aircraft taxied round to the civilian area, where I could disembark and catch the BEA Viscount to London! Overwhelmed, I thanked him profusely, but was still not wholly convinced we would get away with such a dramatic piece of rule-bending. But we did: it all went like clockwork and completely as scheduled. For a Wg. Cdr. to do all this for a lowly National Service SAC was, to my mind, a demonstration of high levels of compassion and duty: he would never have made an MP! My seven weeks' leave went all too quickly. People said I had changed, and they were right! When I returned to Nicosia I found that the EOKA trouble had waned again so that I was able to go back to Episkopi in 'civvies' and didn't have to do my special agent bit again. Several people to whom I've related this adventure found it difficult to believe, but it's true, every word of it.

During my time at HQ MEAF I needed to study for a Civil Service exam and once again I was given exceptionally good treatment, this time by the Flt. Lt. and Plt. Off. i/c the Education section. These two worthies seemed overjoyed that they actully had someone who wanted to learn and proceeded to give me virtually individual tuition. They sent to London for old exam papers and made me sit them under exam conditions. They insisted that I sit a relevant

GCE subject and when I did I finished top in the whole RAF. Back in England, trained to a hair, I took the Civil Service Executive exam and finished 26th in the written part and an overall 2nd following the comprehensive interview. I put this success, which I count as one of the highlights of my life, almost solely down to my RAF experience, since I fear that I would have lacked the self-discipline to do the required work had I been a civilian.

My leave over, I quickly got back into the swing of things. Life was made a little easier when the father of one of my best friends on camp was posted to Cyprus by the Foreign Office and John and I spent some very pleasant weekends with his parents. I entered and failed an officers' aptitude test. I spent a weekend at the Troodos Recreation Camp, where I tried to ski for the first and only time in my life! On the return journey our Greek Cypriot driver was drunk on Ouzo and we had to spend the night in an Army camp half way down the mountain. Our regard for the hitherto-despised 'brown jobs' improved considerably, especially when they let us fire a few rounds on their indoor range. Then we received a polite invitation from the Navy, whose carrier *HMS Ark Royal* was moored outside Limassol harbour. However, they neglected to tell HQ that they expected us in uniform and on the day we were the only ones in civvies! They still let us on board, however, and it was a wonderful experience.

For some time I was content to stay on camp in my free time, there being so much to do. My friends would come back with lurid tales of the Turkish Quarter and my not very well-concealed scepticism eventually led to a challenge, so that one day I found myself going with them. I saw things which I would not have believed possible, principally involving a large Turkish woman, and this despite the fact that my suburban naiveté had been shattered on my very first guard duty when the two Turkish Auxiliary policemen got out their photos! I found out only about three years ago that the café we used to frequent was only a few yards from Grivas' underground hideout! I also acquired a few pen pals, a very rewarding pastime. One, an American girl, thought that SAC stood for Strategic Air Command!

Finally it was time for demob. and home. I've always had a bit of a jackdaw complex, and had accumulated a huge amount of 'gash' equipment. This I put into a room-sized packing-case, addressed it home and trusted it to the gods. It arrived three months after I did — it had been opened, but not a thing had been touched! The RAF, with customary efficiency, repatriated me on the button on 21

August 1958. Once again it was a DC-6 charter flight to Southend, where Customs turned a blind eye to our suitcases full of contraband! I was actually demobbed through RAF Hendon, and within a few days was back in the Ministry of Pensions & National Insurance, a culture shock in reverse!

❑ Mr. Michael Eames (2748542)

After basic training at RAF Padgate, an odd mix of trade training at RAF Middle Wallop and RAF Hereford and some flitting about during a rail strike, I was posted to RAF Laarbruch, near the Dutch border. There I rose to the dizzy eminence of SAC i/c priority spares in the technical equipment section. As a trained radio and TV engineer, I originally aimed at fighter plotting activities, but that is how I contrived to end up.

It was a happy time for me in Germany. My only regret has been the loss of a very good friend, Heinz Manske, who was an interpreter for the Station (of which Gp. Capt. Petre was the Commander) and lived in the nearby town of Goch. I had a few letters from the family in 1957, then total silence. In his last letter, he hinted at a 'problem', but, try as I might, I could never find out what happened to them. I contacted the German Welfare Organisation, but there was nothing they could do. Something untoward happened to the family; I'd still like to know what transpired all those years ago.

❑ Mr. Peter Elms (2770305)

To tell of my National Service experiences forty years on is both a joy and an opportunity to relive days which the passage of time has dimmed. The tedious and aggravating duties, the good times and memories, come flooding back.

Having completed an apprenticeship in 1955 at the age of twenty, I was duly called for National Service, not of course having any conception of the experiences that were ahead. My RAF service commenced, with many other young men, by enlisting at RAF Cardington. From there I went to RAF West Kirby, on the Wirral, for basic training. On our first leave I went with some new-found friends across the Mersey into Liverpool, and being keen football supporters we found our way to Anfield to see Liverpool, at the time a First Division team, play. A week later, we made the same journey, this time to Everton. The distance from my home in Surrey restricted travel possibilities, and it was the end of basic training before a visit home was possible.

From West Kirby I was posted to RAF Catterick to be trained as a signaller/gunner in the RAF Regiment. The Yorkshire moors around nearby Richmond were very bleak and quite desolate, but I remember our training NCOs having one or two good spots sorted out, especially one venue where delicious apple pies could be bought. They were good!

Training over, I was sent to RAF Innsworth, Gloucester, the venue for kitting-out and preparation for overseas service, and then to Blackbushe Airport, where we boarded a civilian Hermes airliner for the Middle East. Due to range limitations, a stop at Malta was necessary. I recall the warm sultry night, and the air with a distinctive smell one feels is characteristic of the Middle East. We used an old Nissen hut converted into a transit building at Luqa, so different from the splendid new airport buildings now serving many thousands of holiday-makers every year. Then on to Cyprus, a jewel in the Mediterranean. RAF Nicosia was the transit camp and I can remember the warmth of the early May sun, a sun we would enjoy for the remainder of our service careers. We were able to get a brief glimpse of the lovely old city of Nicosia by acting as volunteer armed escorts on taxis carrying Station personnel. Officers and NCOs lived in and around Nicosia, and due to the EOKA troubles movement around the island was severely restricted. One Sunday morning some of us quietly left camp on the pretext of carrying out this task, but in reality to visit a family up in the hills and to partake of a sumptuous breakfast, complete with Cypriot brandy, and to enjoy the warmth and generous hospitality of very kind people.

After a very pleasant stay in Cyprus we flew to RAF El Adem in Libya, which was to be our final posting. El Adem was an airfield in the desert some 17 miles south of Tobruk, and was used as a staging post for aircraft flying to and from bases in the Middle East and beyond. On arrival, we asked how far it was to the camp, to be told "This is it!". As 62 Field Sqdn. we were to provide airfield security and to clear wartime mines. Our early days in Libya were spent in routine exercises and experience of living in hostile desert conditions. The area around the Station was still heavily mined, and these weapons laid on the sand over distances of many miles created a most inhospitable area

The Station, which comprised the usual hangars and operational buildings, had a limited number of permanent buildings for accommodation, a NAAFI and a cinema, but the RAF Regt. always lived under canvas. On our first Sunday we saw the temperature rise to 130 F! Working days finished at 13.00 hours,

leaving time for recreation, and transport was provided to allow visits to the beach at Tobruk for what was to become almost a daily routine. Tobruk had been prominent in the desert campaign during the war, which had resulted in near-dereliction from the pounding it received from both sides. Our early days were without incident as we had the town of Tobruk and on weekend passes we could travel along the coast road to Derna, some 120 miles away, where there was some good shopping to be done at very attractive prices. A lasting memory is of an expedition to the desert town of Jaghbub, where we were able to visit the tombs of the Kings of Libya.

While we were on one of these weekend visits the 'quiet revolution' in which King Idris was deposed took place. The President of Egypt, Col. Nasser, then began to gain prominence, and this was the beginning of the changes we were to experience. A strike by Israel on Egyptian airfields brought about the Suez operation, and as a unit close to the border we were put on immediate standby. It was feared that the Egyptian forces would seek to take El Adem as a reprisal. The next twenty-four hours or so consisted of a series of events which began with mobile units moving out into the desert to encircle the airfield, supported by the Station's Shackleton reconnaissance aircraft. The team to which I was attached was out almost all night. Next day the Squadron was ordered out of camp again, and this time our duty was to dig in and to secure all vehicles below ground level, followed by ourselves! Then we waited. Was there to be an invasion? In the event, there was not, but we had a brief experience of the conditions which had faced the 8th Army during the war.

After this episode life returned to normal. An excursion into the desert on one occasion brought us to Sidi Barrani, where one of the fiercest tank battles of the Second World War had taken place. To experience desert travel is unlike anything else — the raging heat of the sun during the day and the cold at night so intense that heavy clothing is essential. Once on the way back to base we met a Bedouin tribe. One of the little girls had a very serious leg injury which we considered needed hospital treatment, but our offer of help was rejected in the belief that Allah would take care of her and his wish would prevail. I often wondered what came of her.

As a boy I was fortunate to learn to play the piano, not serious classics but well enough to enjoy the popular music of the time. I was therefore called upon now and then by our NCOs to provide music in their mess. One night quite late we were all bedded down when our Warrant Officer arrived and asked me to join the party at the mess, emphasisng that it was not an order, just a request. I was pleased to have the opportunity, as by custom a drink was always on the piano! This was my first experience of playing without, at the end of the evening, actually hearing what I was playing! Afterwards, I didn't feel at all well, but as the invitation was repeated those present must have enjoyed the party.

We didn't have the leisure facilities which those back home were beginning to enjoy in the mid-fifties, such as television, and when not on duty we created our own entertainment. The NAAFI was the main centre of social activity and supplemented the mess for food and drink. Our cinema was first-class, with up-to-date films on show. Visiting entertainers sometimes appeared, among them the very popular singer Ruby Murray. We had facilities for most sports, and although there was no swimming pool transport was always avalable to take us to the excellent beach at Tobruk. Winter was not cold, but late autumn brought rain, which washed over the desert without consideration for those under canvas!

During a leave taken at the small town of Derna, an opportunity arose to travel further west to Benghazi on a vehicle of 5001 Squadron. We didn't want to miss this, as the terrain around El Adem and Derna was barren and we hoped to see something different. The route did pass through a fertile region dating from the pre-war Italian influence, where we saw animals living in the houses and the Arabs living in tents outside! On the road we met two Arabs dressed as in Biblical times, on their way to Mecca, carrying wooden ploughs. On arrival at Benghazi we settled into the Salvation Army hostel and set about seeing the town, only to be approached by MPs who told us that our squadron had been given movement orders and we were to return to El Adem at once. Transport was sent for us, but on arrival we found that the orders had been cancelled! We then decided to complete our leave, but never returned to Benghazi.

El Adem was a busy airfield, with many movements of Canberras and the graceful and then-new Vulcan and Valliant heavy bombers. A site had been selected in the desert for a bombing target to be built, under the control of RAF El Adem. A problem arose when our Arab friends used to wait by the target and make off with the empty bomb cases! This resulted in our squadron being called upon to secure the area, including the settlement known as 'Hell's Acre', where we enjoyed many hours of duty. For a time the first De Havilland Comet transport of the RAF was based at El Adem for testing in a hot climate, and we were sometimes allowed on test flights as passengers.

There was little call for ceremonial duties at El Adem, but a guard of honour for the impending visit of Vice-President Nixon was an exception. Days were spent preparing our kit and rehearsing for the big day, but with the airmen at the peak of their performance the visit was called off! The parade would without doubt have been one of the highlights of our short but adventurous service careers.

A combined services venture at sea was an interesting experience for us. The drama began in the port of Benghazi when the British freighter *Empire Chub*, carrying a valuable cargo of British army vehicles, was the subject of great interest by the Egyptian authorities. Its Captain chose to make a run for the open sea after becoming suspicious of armed Libyan guards on the quayside. His courage in easing the ship out of port was to bring us into the episode. We were drafted in with the army to sail with HMS Jamaica on a reconnaissance along the coast to search for the *Empire Chub*. In the morning the news was that Capt. Harvey had sailed safely into Grand Harbour, Malta, his cargo intact.

My lasting memory is of the cemeteries around Tobruk, which are tended with care as a lasting memorial to those men of many nations who fought in the hostile desert environment which later became my home for eighteen months. I also remember the companionship and friendship I found among my friends of the RAF Regiment.

❑ Mr. V. S. Sedwell (2772835)

As I served a civilian apprenticeship, my call-up was deferred until I had completed that and my associated college studies. By the time I reported to RAF Cardington on 5 October 1955 I was aged 22, married, with a son.

We were at Cardington barely a week being kitted out and processed. The only clear recollection I have of it is the two vast hangars built to house the R.100 and R.101 airships. We were grouped into entries and assigned to a School of Recruit Training. My 'luck' was to be sent to RAF Hednesford on Cannock Chase — not too bad a place, as it turned out. On arrival there we were told to leave the coach and pile our kit at the side of the road, and were then formed up and our names checked before we were assigned to Flights, huts etc. At this point the officer who had been supervising this stage of the proceedings departed, and we were left to the mercy of the Drill Instructors. These seemed to go demented, screaming at us to get our kit within ten seconds and be back in our newly-allocated Flight or face a charge! All bluff, of course, but to a group of young men in a strange environment it was terrifying.

The next two weeks were pure hell. I was appointed Senior Man in my billet, partly because I was comparatively old compared to the 18-year-olds and also I had previous service in the Army Cadets and TA. During the early stage we were subjected to snap kit inspections and for the most trivial reasons kit was thrown out of the billet window to be prepared again. I quickly discovered that as Senior man I was spared such humiliations but instead I was bawled out for everything that was considered not up to standard in the billet and was made to ensure that I got the others to put things right. I don't know which was worse — it made for strained relations in the billet at times.

The third week of 'square-bashing' was fatigues week and each of the four Squadrons on the camp did all the dirty jobs on a rota basis. These were mainly cookhouse duties, with some cleaning and painting jobs around the camp. Luckily I had a chum one week ahead of me who told me to volunteer for Church cleaning duties. This I did, and had the cushiest week of the time I spent at Hednesford. Each morning with another airman from my billet (who I had also tipped off) I reported to the RC Chapel and did some light dusting. Next door was the Catholic Social Club, where we arranged the papers and then spent the day reading and making coffee. All the rest of our Entry were coming back to the billet worn out and filthy — what a lucky escape we had!

In the fourth week a change started to come over our DIs. They began to become more relaxed and have a bit of fun and a joke. The DI directly responsible for my Flight was a Cpl. Elliott, an unusual character. He was an economics graduate who had suffered a nervous breakdown shortly after completing his degree exams and had been advised to take a long break from further academic study. As he was due for call-up anyway he promptly signed on for five years as a DI — one couldn't get anything less academic than that! His room at the end of the billet was also unusual; instead of the normal pin-ups it was lined with books on economics, and in my latter weeks at Hednesford he would invite me in some evenings for a chat about the problems of the day.

Other recollections of Hednesford include the best mixed grill of my life, put on specially by the Flt. Sgt. cook, who put in the biggest steak, several eggs, sausages and rashers of bacon. I had been on late duty and missed the regular 'high tea'. It tasted wonderful, and made me modify my views on Flight Sergeants!

In our billet there was a young Jewish boy named Michael Rose. He was always in trouble with the DIs, the RAF Regiment NCOs and just about everyone he came into contact with. The trouble was that he came from a wealthy family and had never had to do anything for himself. He had always had a maid or butler to even dress him! It became a problem to us because he always seemed to be on 'jankers' and as a result was subject to extra kit inspections. This was a nuisance to all in the billet because just as we were trying to relax of an evening there was a sudden cry of "Officer present" and we all had to jump to attention while Michael had his kit inspected. After the first spell of this we all rallied round to help get his kit up to standard, to get him up in the morning (one of the reasons he kept going on 'jankers'), and to inspect him before he went out. It was really self-preservation by ourselves. When he returned to camp after the long weekend leave half-way through the training, his mother brought him in a chauffer-driven Rolls-Royce! I often wonder what happened to him; I imagine he runs a merchant bank or suchlike now.

At 'square-bashing' I found that the worst NCOs were those of the RAF Regiment, far worse than the DIs. They organised our ground combat training, and I well remember two freezing nights on Cannock Chase in November 1955. It was impossible to sleep, and all day we were harrassed and bullied by the awful 'Rock Apes'.

I had asked to be trained as an Instrument Technician (General), an advanced trade for which I was eligible by reason of my apprenticeship and having an Ordinary National Certificate. It was fortunate that the next Direct Entry course was not due to start at RAF Melksham until January, so when we passed out from Hednesford in early December I got an extended leave. The passing-out parade was one of the proudest moments of my life. On that day I think we would have done credit to the Brigade of Guards!

On 27 December 1955 I reported to 12 SoTT, RAF Melksham. We were to relieve a skeleton staff of 'Jocks' so that they could go home for Hogmanay, and we spent the next few days on guard duty. Immediately after the New Year I started my 35-week course. It was very tough but interesting and I still have a high regard for the thoroughness of the training given by the RAF. I was in Entry DE361, and out of the 25 of us only two were regulars, both three-year men. One of us had a degree, most had HNCs — my ONC was quite modest by comparison. We all 'gelled' very well together. Being ex-apprentices we were all older than the typical NS men.

Life at Melksham was quite relaxed after 'square-bashing'. The only incident that stands out was my being charged for skipping working parade, something that most did. I was unlucky to get caught, and lucky to get off with a reprimand. We had a WRAF Corporal PTI who was determined that we were all going to learn to play a ball-game, and mine was to be tennis. I don't think I ever hit the ball once! In September 1956 I passed out as a J/T Instrument Fitter (General). We were known as 'Australian Lance-Jacks' because our badge of rank was a single inverted stripe.

What a passing-out night! Apart from wrecking our own billet, we let off fire extinguishers in the adjacent huts. Not an episode I'm terribly proud of but we were young and exuberant I suppose.

Most of my Entry went overseas, Singapore and Aden mainly. I volunteered to go, so they posted me to RAF Chivenor in north Devon! This illustrates the perversity of the RAF postings authority. I arrived at Chivenor on a hot summer day with hordes of visitors — it was the annual Battle of Britain open day! I'd been told to go straight from Melksham to Chivenor and not be tempted to divert home for the weekend as RAF Chivenor was expecting me. What lies! In my youthful naivity I believed them, but in fact they knew nothing about me and didn't seem particularly pleased to see me on what was one of their most hectic days of the year. My paperwork didn't arrive until the following Wednesday.

While in this state of limbo, I was sent off to help guard a Vampire aircraft which had crashed near Tiverton, killing the Iraqi pilot. The engine had been ripped from the fuselage, taking the pilot with it into a wood. The sight revolted me and I felt quite ill for several days. Chivenor was the home of 229 OCU, and trained qualified pilots to become fighter pilots. Some of the trainees came from overseas, including, during my stay, quite a number from Iraq. Rather ironic in the light of more recent events in the Gulf. I expect that one or two of our trainees found themselves fighting against us as senior Iraqi Air Force officers. They were a hopeless bunch, with poor navigational skills, always getting lost and running out of fuel, which is what had happened to the one I went to guard. Of all the crashes that occured while I was at Chivenor I can only think of one that didn't involve an Iraqi!

My time at Chivenor was spent mainly in the calibration room of Technical Wing HQ. I was kept fairly busy, working mostly on my own. My Flight Sergeant had an office just off the calibration room where he conducted a thriving watch repair business! As long as I kept him free of problems he was content to leave me alone. Better still, he gave me a standing authority to have early meals or late meals as I wished. Very useful!

Chivenor while I was there went through a transition from Vampire aircraft to Hunters. There was also a Search & Rescue helicopter Flight from 22 Sqdn. on detachment. This gave me a wide range of instruments to work on.

Guard duty at Chivenor was not without its amusing incidents. On one of my early spells of duty I discovered a loose window in one of the Flight offices. This gave access to the instructors' room, where they brewed their tea and coffee. Thereafter my two-hour stints were passed, along with a fellow guard, pleasantly drinking the instructors' coffee and eating their biscuits. We nearly got caught when the Orderly Officer came snooping round and shone his torch through the window full in my face! My companion and I just froze and by some miracle the officer didn't see us! If he had I should think it would have been a court martial for us.

While I was at Chivenor one unfortunate individual was court-martialled. As always at an RAF Station, there was great pressure to get all aircraft declared serviceable in the morning as quickly as possible. In order to do this the ground crews took all sorts of short cuts in pre-flight checks. One of these was for the armament mechanic to sit in the cockpit to act as brake-man while the aircraft was towed out. This enabled him to do his checks while the aircraft was in motion, including checking the firing button mounted on the joy-stick. This was strictly against the rules and unfortunately for the poor mechanic the four cannon on the Hunter had not been cleared properly and each still had one round in the breech. As soon as he pressed the firing button the cannons roared into life. The Land Rover towing the Hunter just disintegrated, leaving the driver sitting on a bare chassis but mercifully with only a minor flesh wound to one arm. Two aircraft parked on the apron had holes in them! A lot of people got one hell of a fright and the armament mechanic had to be carried off in a dead faint. At the subsequent Court Martial it turned out that so many people, including SNCOs, had not done all they should that he got off with 28 days guardroom detention. He had been confined to the guardroom for about a month anyway by the time his case was heard so he was out almost at once. A very salutory lesson to us all — there but for the grace of God go I! I was always nervous when Form 700s were impounded following a crash — had I signed for anything I shouldn't?

Towards the end of my time I was tempted to sign on, indeed for several years after my demob. I was tempted to go back, but my first wife was strongly opposed to the idea so I never did. Recently I attended the unveiling of a commemorative stone at the site of RAF Melksham, which closed in 1964, and all the memories came flooding back. I enjoyed nearly all my time in the RAF and would not have missed it for the world. I feel proud to have been part of a great Service and, given my time over again, even knowing what I know now, I would still be tempted to sign on!

❏ Mr. R. Mann (2778274)

As a National Serviceman, I considered myself very lucky, firstly in being taken into the RAF, which was unusual at the time, secondly by getting the trade I wanted, which was almost unheard of, and thirdly by getting an exchange poating to a different Command (Coastal to Fighter) at a Station fairly close to home.

I reported to RAF Cardington on 21 November 1955 for kitting out and then went to RAF Weeton for a trade test. My 'square-bashing' was at RAF West Kirby, from where I passed out on 6 February 1956. After the usual leave I was posted to RAF St. Mawgan in Cornwall to work at RAF Falmouth air-sea rescue unit, but I managed to secure the exchange posting to RAF Biggin Hill in June 1956. My trade was MT driver/mechanic, and I managed to write off one staff car during my service! On demobilisation on 20 November 1957 I had reached the rank of SAC.

❏ Mr. A. L. Goodwin (2787856)

On 20 February 1956 I reported to RAF Cardington, where I spent a week being kitted out etc. We were then sent to RAF West Kirby for 'square-bashing', and passed out at the end of April. My trade selection was Clerk/Typist, so I was posted to RAF Credenhill, near Hereford, which was then the RAF School of Admin. Training. After twelve weeks we received our postings — to Cyprus. You might imagine our apprehension at this, because at the time Cyprus was in the throes of the EOKA terrorist campaign.

We arrived in Cyprus in the middle of September 1956. Cyprus was in Middle East Air Force Command, the HQ of which was at Episkopi, in the south of the island. The C-in-C at the time was Air Marshal Sir Dermot Boyle. We were based at Air Headquarters Levant, situated within the site of RAF Nicosia, which included Nicosia airport, five miles west of the town.

At the end of September 1956 the Suez crisis hit us. We were accommodated in unused married quarters bungalows about half a mile from the airfield and I can remember watching Canberra bombers taking off and heading south. Later in the evening we knew why when the bombing of Egypt was announced on the news.

Although we were aware of terrorist activities, we were never directly involved in any incidents. A partial truce in February 1957 allowed us to tour the island. We were awarded the General Service Medal for the Cyprus campaign. I was 'demobbed' in February 1958.

[Editor's note: Very soon after Mr. Goodwin entered the RAF on 20 February 1956, the end of a batch of service numbers, 2787999, was reached, and before Mr. Jackson arrived at Cardington three days later another batch had begun at 5010251. About 400 non-ATC entrants appear, therefore, to have joined in those three days.]

❏ Mr. Peter F. Jackson (5010477)

I was eighteen and a half years old when I was called up and remember arriving at RAF Cardington by train from my home town of Bristol via London on a very cold day. I also recall that on the coach which met us at Bedford station the Sergeant urged us to sign on for three years, as that way we would be allowed out of camp early on. I don't think there were any takers!

Cardington was a shock, with wooden huts, each housing about 22 people and a Corporal who had a small room at the end and whom we hardly saw except when he scurried to get fuel for his stove. He seemed very old, probably about fifty. We had our jabs, collected our kit, sent our 'civvies' home, learnt how to make a bed, were again subjected to the sales talk about signing on, and then got our postings to our 'square-bashing' camps. I suppose we all disappeared in different directions to those camps, but I only remember the long coach ride to RAF Hednesford, on Cannock Chase in Staffordshire. Each 'square-bashing' camp had its own reputation, and Hednesford was not quite the fiercest; RAF West Kirby had that distinction, and there had been a suicide there not long before, but Hednesford was bad enough. It was an enormous shock to most of us, the exceptions being two men who had previously served in the Army and the Navy, and were quite used to the treatment we had. It was very cold and water froze in the taps in the ablutions, making washing and shaving difficult.

I seem to remember always being tired, and the lights going out in the hut at 21.30, as we were awakened each morning at 05.30 by a screaming

NCO. We acclimatised fairly quickly, though, particularly as each week another batch of recruits arrived and we must have heard the slogan "Get some in" at around that time. Some sort of esprit de corps built up, and I seem to recall that the Flight I was in, (D Flight, 22 Squadron), was a good one, and we did pretty well at the various tests we had to do as a Flight. Highlights (or lowlights) were walking around the gas chamber singing "The Happy Wanderer" before taking off our gas masks and spluttering as the gas was released; the R&I camp somewhere in the middle of Cannock Chase, where we spent an exciting three days playing soldiers; the food in the cookhouse, which was awful and had to be supplemented by visits to the NAAFI; a variety show put on for us by some fairly dead-beat entertainers, either young ones on the way up or old ones on the way down, but with plenty of tailor-made jokes about our Corporals and SPs, which we appreciated; and the passing-out parade, which was pretty stirring.

I had been given the trade of typist, having failed to get on an officer training course, though, having a few O-levels I was briefly a POM (Potential Officer Material). Only about a dozen of us POMs actually made it to the OCTU at Jurby, and I think we were really quite relieved.

Trade training was at RAF Credenhill, near Hereford, where the regime was much milder, though we still had some drill and PT. Most of the time was spent on the RAF's crash course in typing, which did in twelve weeks what a civilian course would have taken at least six months to do. Instructors were middle-aged Corporals and Sergeants who probably joined the RAF years before for the glamour of the life and ended up teaching typing! Actually, it was a very useful skill to learn and more use in later years than most trades. Two memories stand out, neither dramatic or unusual. Returning from a 36-hour pass, I got on the wrong part of the train at Bristol and watched the right part moving out, with me stuck immobile. I got back to camp about eight hours late at 08.00 next morning, was hauled up before the SWO, given a lecture about the folly of waiting until the last train back to camp and told that the Adjutant might wish to see me during the day and that I would be summoned over the tannoy. I spent the whole day waiting for the announcement, which never came. I got off because I had been to the RTO at the station for a 'chitty' certifying that I had been misdirected onto the wrong bit of train! On getting back (on time) from another 36, I found that heavy rain had flooded our hut, which was at the bottom of a slight gradient, and we had to dismantle everything, clear the hut and move to another one, get what sleep we could and then do a day's training next day.

Most of our course passed the final trade test, and we dispersed to our next postings, which were pretty well all over the world, including Cyprus, Aden, Hong Kong, and in my case Germany. We were threatened with RAF Habbaniya, Iraq, the usual service threat which came to nothing. I was quite pleased with Germany, as I had done German to 'A' Level at school, though in retrospect a posting further away would have been more exciting. After a week's embarkation leave, I had to get to Liverpool St. station to get the troop train for Harwich, along with hundreds of others going to Germany for the first time or returning from leave. We sailed on the *Empire Wansbeck*, which was probably a death trap, with troops berthed below the water line in bunks two or three high set very close together. I hate to think what the crossing was like in the winter. We landed at the Hook of Holland, and were shoved into a huge shed where breakfast was given to us, and then we were off on a troop train across Holland to RAF Goch, a transit camp just inside Germany for one night while we received our postings. A few from the course at Credenhill were still together at that stage, but we all split up after Goch and I was told that I was going to 755 Signals Unit at some place called Hambühren which they couldn't find on the map, so all I was told was that I should go as far as Celle and hope someone from the camp met the train. Luckily one other airman was also going to Hambühren. I don't remember much about the journey except that it was rather dreary, through the Ruhr and then the flat country around Hanover, but we duly arrived at Celle at about 22.00 in heavy rain and were met at the station by a Volkswagen Kombi, a sort of minibus used a lot by the forces in Germany.

We had two surprises on reaching the camp at Hambühren, which at that time was a small village about six miles from Celle, where there was a much larger RAF operational Station. The first was that when we reported to the guardroom we were invitied inside and given a hot meal and treated in a very friendly fashion, quite unlike the way the SPs had always behaved towards us during training. The second surprise was that the airmen's accommodation was in centrally-heated brick-built barrack blocks with rooms containing no more than four beds, a luxurious change after the 22-bed wooden huts of the UK.

It was a small camp for 200 men, built before the war for the German Army, and it was not a flying Station, but involved in intelligence gathering, so we had to sign the Official Secrets Act and to have security clearance. The camp was quite close to the Belsen concentration camp, and it was odd to see buses with the sign Bergen-Belsen going past to the nearby village. On the whole it was a good posting, because there was very little drill, few parades and not much 'bull'. German civilians employed by the German Service Organisation cleaned the corridors, ablutions and stairs, worked as gardeners and manned the main gate, though we had to keep our rooms clean, with 'bull' night on Monday evenings taking all of half an hour. Inspections were few and fairly lenient.

I worked as a typist in SHQ, pounding away on heavy manual typewriters and getting to know a lot of what was happening, because everything had to be typed and the typist was therefore a central figure. Occasionally there would be a court martial, with stacks of typing of documents, but the main chore was the weekly Station Routine Orders (SROs), edited by the Adjutant and giving duty lists such as fire picquet, orderly officer, orderly Sergeant, duty clerk (I had to take a turn at that), anything important from the Air Ministry that the troops should know about, and the regular repeating of certain orders at prescribed intervals.

Looking back, I regret that I didn't take the chance to use my spare time, such as the odd 48-hour pass, to travel a bit in Germany, rather than going to Celle, or once or twice to Hanover, but I think the real reason was that we had very little money. Pay was only £4 or so a week, and that didn't leave much for anything other than short trips, and of course any surplus cash was saved for UK leave, flying at a special troop rate on BEA of about £26. Some of the more adventurous people, such as the rather better-paid J/Ts, did go to the south of Germany in winter to ski, but that was beyond most of us.

I remember an RAF Station at Fassberg, a few miles north of us, closing down, and a convoy of trucks going there from Hambühren to 'liberate' some of the furniture. One of the drivers was in my room, and we suddenly became exceedingly well furnished!

In some ways, the camp was a satellite of RAF Celle, using some of its sports facilities, its churches, and collecting its mail from there every day, but our camp had a small cinema, furnished with an odd assortment of seats, including a large sofa, for which the charge was 1/6 (7.5p.) compared with the cheap seats at 1/- (5p.). We saw some terrible films as the best ones went to the Army Globe Kinema in Celle. We had a sports field and played cricket and football against other units, including the army.

There was little contact with the German people, and apparently no official attempt was made to link the camp with the locality. I don't remember any hostility towards us, and I suppose even our limited spending power contributed to the German economic miracle which was gathering pace at the time.

After a few months, I was transferred from SHQ to the top security block, having been given a higher security clearance, but the work was not so interesting. The main benefit was that I was regarded as being on essential duties and so avoided the few parades that were held. In October 1957 the camp was handed over to the re-formed Luftwaffe and we all left. The whole camp transferred itself down the autobahn to 477 Signals Unit at RAF Butzweilerhof, near Cologne. This was a very different place. It was a flying Station, with Vampires and Venoms, and also had us, the British army and the Belgian army, but it also had facilities we had lacked at Hambühren such as a Malcolm Club, a proper cinema, a good library (I was studying for professional exams at the time), and it was near Cologne, which was a good place to visit. The regime was a bit tougher, though nothing compared with the Army's, and we did have weekly parades which had to be taken by our officers from Hambühren, who plainly didn't want to!

This was the nearest I ever came to an aircraft, and then only at a distance as our unit was a long way from the runways, and I wonder how many airmen actually had anything to do with aircraft. Because the two units I served on after training were small, we had officers of lower ranks than on larger units. The COs of Signals Units were Squadron Leaders, and the Adjutants were Flying Offciers, and the only time I saw anyone of a higher rank was at the passing-out parade at Hednesford, taken by the CO, who was a Group Captain. There was a CO at RAF Butzweilerhof, also a Group Captain, but we never saw him!

After four months at 'Butz', my repat date, as it was called, came through and I went back on the troop train from the Hook to Harwich and then to RAF Innsworth for the final few days and 'demob', which we all welcomed, cheering loudly as we were driven out of the camp in the back of a truck to Cheltenham station.

My time was uneventful, with no danger, no sign of any action apart from the occasional flap at the time of Suez and the Hungarian revolution in 1956, when we thought we might be sent somewhere else, but I look back on two years with a lot of nostalgia and keep in regular touch with three others who served at Hambühren.

❏ Mr. C. Hutchinson (3149431)

My RAF service began on 18 April 1956 at Cardington for kitting-out, but my most vivid memories of Air Force life started on the day we arrived at RAF Hednesford and the reception we received form the Corporal DIs of 'A' Squadron. We were all, quite honestly, absolutely terrified! Gradually we got used to the unbelievably strict discipline and settled down to 'spit-and-polishing' our boots, shrinking our oversized berets in hot and cold water, taking needles in the arm, firing on the range, learning how to tie knots (what for I don't know!), endless drill and PT, and intelligence tests. We went on trips to Birmingham at weekends, and I remember walking in a park with a sixteen-year-old girl. I never saw her again and have often wondered what happened to her. Then it was goodbye to Corporals West, Williams and Enis and postings to trade training, in my case to RAF Kirkham, near Blackpool, where I was a member of 58 Entry.

Life at Kirkham was dead easy. Somehow about twenty of us found ourselves in a billet which seemed to have been forgotten by the camp authorities. We had no Corporal or any intervention by anybody. Making the most of our freedom, we decided not to bother about sweeping up, and chucked newspapers on the billet floor. We never made our beds and in general the place became a perfect pigsty. This went on for about three weeks, until one fine morning the door opened and in walked a Corporal and a Sergeant. Down the billet they stalked and out the other end without uttering a word. We all laid back on our 'pits' aghast at what was to follow. The very next day a Corporal was assigned to the room at the end of the billet, after which we had a more difficult time.

At Kirkham it was mainly book-work — maths, English and science. We had redundant Supermarine Swifts to practice on and it was a very agreeable place to be that summer before the Suez crisis. On Wednesday afternoons we went into Blackpool in buses laid on by the RAF. Three of us would pool our money, about eighteen shillings (90p.) all told, which was enough for a meal and a pint and a late bus back to Kirkham! Then came the trade tests, which involved a written paper and a walk around a hangar full of dismantled aircraft, with questions about this and that being fired at us by a Flight Sergeant instructor. The following week was spent on fatigues around the camp while all the talk was of postings. One rumour said that we were all going to Germany. No, it's Singapore and Malaya, said another. In fact we were all split up and went our different ways. About half the Entry finished up on troopships going to every Station from Gibraltar to Hong Kong, but I went to RAF Cranwell as an airframe mechanic.

I expected Cranwell to be a strict high-discipline posting, but it was not really too bad. We had the usual panic for AOC's inspection, and early morning parade rehearsals in the frost, with bayonets fixed, but in general the theme was to to keep the aircraft rolling out. I remember once finding some hairline fractures on the tailplane of a Vampire training aircraft. Within an hour all the top engineering 'brass' were crawling all over the aircraft and pointing fingers at me as the 'erk' who had found the problem. Very proud of myself, I was! Aircraft used to 'prang' now and then or go missing over the North Sea. Once the main engine bearing of a two-seat Vampire seized up; the cadet pilot ejected but the instructor stayed with the aircraft in true RAF tradition and was killed.

While doing my stint on crash-crew one Saturday morning there was an alert. The pilot of a two-seat Vampire was unable to get the port wheel down and therefore had to bring the aircraft in for a wheels-up landing. Everyone else at Cranwell had gone off duty for the weekend, and we waited for the crash-landing, intent only on getting the aircraft down so that we too could 'push off'. The callousness of youth! The landing was perfect, and we all charged down the runway after the aircraft. The crew were in the ambulance within seconds.

Another event at Cranwell was the filming of the

HOLLY

movie "High Flight" with Helen Cherry and Ray Milland. A good deal of the filming was done outside our hangar, much to the annoyance of our WO-man, who couldn't get us to do any work.

I was, I'm sorry to say, a bit bored at Cranwell. We had to do overtime if we got behind with servicing the aircraft, and without any extra pay. Our meals would be brought to us by the MT Section.

I have quite a few memories of life in the RAF, mostly good, with the passing of time. I can honestly say that I have never met in 'Civvie Street' such decent guys as I did in the RAF. Perhaps as we were all young we didn't have the hang-ups and misdeeds of later life to colour our proportion of things.

❏ Mr. Terence Chapman (5011038)

From 12 to 20 July 1956 I was at RAF Cardington being kitted out and having trade interviews before being sent to RAF Hednesford for two months' basic training. There I underwent the usual discipline, and little of interest occured except that when we were out on Cannock Chase our tents at Beaudesert were flooded one night, bringing the exercise to a rapid conclusion after a single day. Six weeks trade training as a Clerk/Accounts was carried out at RAF Credenhill, after which I was posted to RAF Honiley as a clerk handling civilian employees' pay and domestic bills for married quarters. In addition, I had responsibility for the petrol coupons issued during the Suez crisis. I was at Honiley until June 1957, when I was posted to RAF Duxford to do similar work.

While at Duxford I took part in Battle of Britain day activities by participating in a stunt involving a scene from the book '1984' in which we were dressed up as civil defence forces, armed with fire extinguishers and had to drive away Martians who had landed and were armed with thunderflashes. I used to cycle around the Cambridgeshire countryside until my three-speed gear and cycle chain were stolen! I found that motorists were very willing to give lifts to airmen in uniform, so I used to hitch-hike to London and back.

I thought when I entered the RAF, and still think now, that I could have spent my time better by getting on with my career. The Forces had too much manpower, and this was acknowledged by the ending of National Service from 1960. Even so, there might be a case now for introducing a certain form of national service to bring discipline to some of the present younger generation. Apart from petty restrictions, I recall being aggrieved that someone I knew who was a conscientious objector was receiving about £9 per week for working in a hospital while I was getting just over £2!

❏ Mr. C. C. Bebb (5034000)

My service number was 5034000, and I had some difficulty with my 'last three' on pay parade. Eventually I settled for Treble Zero, which was accepted by one and all.

I arrived at RAF Cardington on 10 October 1956. We were taken for a meal, and this is when I first came to see square eggs. About two dozen eggs were fried in a tray and when served were cut into square sections with a congealed yolk in the centre! I arrived with an intake of mostly Welsh countrymen of mine, but fate took a turn in the form of a failed X-Ray, and I found myself back-Flighted in the first week. So instead of training at RAF Padgate with people I knew, I was sent to RAF Wilmslow with a fresh set of friends, 80% of whom were Scottish. A few years ago I wrote a poem entitled 'A National Service Airman Remembers' on the subject of 'square-bashing'[reproduced in Appendix — Ed.].

After training at Wilmslow, and not needing trade training as I was a time-served apprentice motor mechanic, I was posted on 2 January 1957 to RAF West Kirby as permament staff in the MTRS. During this time I met and married my wife. In late January 1958 I was posted to RAF Merryfield, near Taunton in Somerset, where I was to complete my service. During my two years in the RAF I never saw an RAF aircraft other than a gate guardian!

❏ Mr. Duncan Furner (5100003)

After leaving school in December 1955, I, along with all my contemporaries, assumed that we would be called up for National Service at or near our eighteenth birthdays — mine was on 19 April 1957. However, there was a slow-down in conscription due to the gradual phasing-out of National Service and I eventually enlisted on 23 February 1959. The intervening period I spent as an insurance clerk.

My memory of that time is sparse but I do recall the fear and apprehension I felt at the unknown. Although I had spent many holidays apart from my parents I had not 'left home' as such, and the break was painful. I can imagine what it must have been like for my parents, as being a parent myself I know what I went through when my sons left home!

I can remember being seen off at a London railway station en route to RAF Cardington and on arrival recall clearly the barrage balloons tethered at the base. All my kit was marked with my service number, 5012254, but during the week I was there the number was changed to 5100003. Items such as a pair of braces and a belt carried the original number throughout my service. I have in front of me my CCF Record of Service, which shows that I served for three years and three months with Bancroft's School CCF, Woodford Green, Essex and was discharged on 15 December 1955. [This is the reason for the change of number — a new series for ex-cadets was started — see Chapter 1 — Ed.]

Then I was sent to 4 SoRT, RAF Wilmslow, for basic training. What a traumatic experience that was! I must have been quite naive in those days as my eyes were opened very wide indeed in a hut with 21 other young lads! I'd never even heard of black-balling, let alone witnessed the action. I have a photograph of the hut occupants together with the NCO i/c our Flight, Cpl. Machin. He was OK as far as I can remember, but the Corporal in charge of the hut, whose name fortunately escapes me, was a real b*****d! For twenty years of my adult career I held a supervisory rank in the police service, five of them as a basic training Sergeant, and I always had in the back of my mind that I must never treat my officers in the way that Corporal treated his airmen. I know we were all 'green' and needed discipline but there are kind, humane ways of doing it.

Being the months of February to April, the weather was atrocious at times, especially during our training under canvas on Leek Moor. Despite having walked many subsequent miles, I have never suffered since from blisters on the feet as I did during that camp. There were six or seven on each foot — what a memory! Somewhere I have photos of the Flight dangling their feet into an icy stream. Square-bashing with snow falling is another vivid memory, and of course the motherless Corporal would keep us standing to attention for what seemed to be hours at a time. Giving him breakfast in bed every morning is another memory!

Eventually the pain stopped and some time in April 1959 I was posted to 2 School of Admin Trades, RAF Credenhill, Hereford, where I commenced a basic Clerk/General Duties course. I had wanted the trade of air traffic controller but with my office-trained background I got clerking. During the course I realised that I could not subsist for the next two years on a wage of £1-11-6 (£1.57) a week, having been used to earning about £1 a day before being called up. I expect my parents would have subsidised me but I wanted to be independent so I decided to sign on as a regular. Having made enquiries about transferring to the trade of air traffic controller I was told I would have to sign on for nine years! A joke was a joke, but I had in mind three years only! In that event I was offered basic Clerk/Accounting, which sounded a good wheeze

— and so it turned out to be. And it offered a wage of £4-4-0 (£4.20) per week!

[Editor's note: Mr. Furner's subsequent service as a regular is outside the scope of this book].

☐ Mr. Peter Symons (5068989)

5068989! Many details of my National Service in the RAF have been lost in the murky recesses of my mind, but my old service number is still as fresh as the day I was ordered to commit it to memory. It must have been June or July 1959 when I reported to RAF Cardington, Bedfordshire, to be kitted out. All I can remember about that is the huge hangars built for airships and the horribly greasy food.

Then it was on to RAF Bridgnorth in Shropshire for basic training, and thence to RAF Compton Basset, Wiltshire, for trade training as a wireless operator. Do you remember stating on one of the numerous forms that had to be filled in, what job you would like to do in the RAF? I had put down carpenter, for that was what I was, or driver, as that was what I hoped to be taught. But that particular week wireless operators were required, so that is what I became. I had been offered a DI's job at Bridgnorth, which would have meant two stripes and more pay, but it also meant staying there for my two years' service. My financial situation at the time precluded much in the way of foreign travel, so I declined the offer and applied for a foreign posting. At least I would get to see a bit of the world free of charge, but Aden?! Not a country I would have chosen, so it's just as well no choice was offered. And so I went to RAF Innsworth, near Gloucester, to be kitted out, this time with tropical gear.

From there I went in civilian clothes to Heathrow Airport to board a Britannia for the twelve-hour flight to RAF Khormaksar, the main British base in Aden. For me it was only a four-day stay at Khormaksar, then 'up country' to RAF Riyan, a small coastal Station 300 miles to the east. This was the first of the route stations, the others being Salalah, Masirah and Sharjah, all on the coastal route to Bahrein. Apparently, military aircraft were not allowed to fly direct to Bahrein from Aden as this would involve crossing Saudi Arabia. The flight to Riyan was aboard a DC-3 which had seats down one side and crates and sacks of fresh vegetables down the other. On leaving the aircraft, my first thought was "What on earth am I going to do here for a year?" I could see only three or four small buildings, one of which had a sign on the front bearing the legend 'International Airport Riyan, Gateway to Mystic Mukalla'. There was more to the camp, but not much.

I learned later that the full complement on the Station was just 57 RAF personnel, including only two officers, the CO, who was a Flt. Lt., and the Adjutant, a Plt. Off. known as 'Adj.'. My job was operating ground-to-ground morse-code circuits between all the route stations, sending and receiving such traffic as flight plans, encoded messages and general administrative material. Once a day we used to call Mukalla, where there was a unit of the Hadrami Bedouin Legion, in case there were any urgent messages. The atmosphere was very relaxed and informal, and as the weather was always hot most people wore uniform only for pay parades or when somebody important was visiting. Being only a mile or so from the sea, there was usually a good breeze, which kept temperatures from becoming unbearable, although humidity was high. On most days a group of off-duty lads would go to the beach. In the whole of my year at Riyan it rained for only two days. This was enough to soften the hard rolled earth runway to allow a DC-4 of Aden Airways to sink almost up to its axles. It was something of a minor miracle that it did not tip onto its nose. The ancient tarmac runway had long since fallen into disuse, although we did manage to find a sufficiently large pothole-free area on which to race our go-carts.

During the cool season — it wasn't called winter — Combined Services Entertainment groups would visit the route stations. I always thought it wondeful that famous entertainers such as Jewell and Warris and Lorrae Desmond would come to these remote places to perform for tiny audiences. There would always be a party afterwards, and it was at one of them that Bukka, one of our Arab cooks, did a fire-breathing act. Our young Adjutant tried to emulate him, but ended up with burning lighter fuel all over his face. The quick-thinking Corporal from the fire section doused it by throwing a full pint of beer in his face, then wanted to know who was going to pay for the replacement pint! Christmas Day 1960 was celebrated with a soccer match. We played in fancy dress, with three teams, three goals and a rugby ball, and the referee rode a bicycle. We also gave a tea-party for a group of children from a nearby Bedouin camp. Another time, we played a proper soccer match against a team of locals at Mukalla and were soundly beaten!

I did manage to do a little carpentry while at Riyan. The Chief Technician in charge of the cookhouse bought some chickens so that we could have fresh eggs, and I built the hen-house. I also became the camp barber, inheriting a comb, a pair of blunt scissors and hand-operated clippers (also blunt). Once I even cut the Adjutant's hair — that is

to say, some of it was cut, some pulled out by the roots!

Along with thousands of others, I received a medal, the GSM, for being on active service, although I never saw action of any sort. The nearest we came to anything remotely threatening was when two Arab tribes had a feud, and the CO briefed us on what to do if we were attacked. A Shackleton sent from Khormaksar dropped a few bombs further up country, frightening the combatants into calling off their quarrel. The same aircraft brought two wounded tribesmen back to Riyan, one of whom had been stabbed and the other shot five times through one arm. They were taken to a hospital run by UNICEF in Mukalla.

On my return to the UK in January 1961 I had five months to serve, which I spent at RAF Digby, near Lincoln, on boring work — hours and hours of monitoring practically non-existent morse code broadcasts. Digby was reputed to have the best food in the RAF, but it didn't match that served by our

Working Blue... or Best Blue?

Arab cooks at Riyan.

For some time I had recurrent nightmares about not being allowed out of the RAF, and this after I had been demobbed! Yes, we had some laughs, and some serious moments too. I'm glad I went.

☐ Mr. Danny Miller (5076990)

On being called up, I left Scotland on 5 April 1960 to report to RAF Cardington to be kitted out, but for some reason there was not a uniform to fit me, so I walked about camp in denims or 'civvies', which felt strange to say the least.

I was then posted to 7 SoRT at RAF Bridgnorth to do basic training, still without a uniform, but when I arrived I found two other Scotsmen in the same situation so I did not feel so odd. On parade one day, eighty of us were informed that volunteers were wanted, and we were all promptly marched down to the Medical Section to give a pint of blood. Our ear lobes were pricked to test our blood to see whether it was suitable, and one 6'4" chap fainted!

After basic training, I was sent to the Ceremonial Drill Unit at RAF Uxbridge. This unit was taken over in October 1960 by the RAF Regiment and renamed the Queen's Colour Squadron of the Royal Air Force. I had the choice of taking a posting or joining the Regiment. Not knowing which to choose, I tossed a coin and joined the Regiment when the coin came down heads. Two weeks later, I met the girl to whom I have been married for 33 years.

I enjoyed my time as a National Serviceman, and it helped me map out my future life, but it was hard for married men. They only received twelve shillings (£0.60) per week after the wife's allowance had been deducted, and single men 28 shillings (£1.40), so I don't think it was enjoyed by everyone. After six months our pay went up to £2-10-0 (£2.50) and in our last six months to £3-14-0 (£3.70). I thought I was RICH!

☐ Mr. Brian Wyatt (5077958)

Call-up day was 23 May 1960 at RAF Cardington, followed by transfer after uniform issue to RAF Bridgnorth. National Servicemen were at this time issued with two uniforms — one 'working blue' and one ' best blue', though in fact they were identical.

The highlight of basic training was that after six weeks we were moved to RAF West Drayton/Uxbridge to provide route-lining troops for the visit of the King of Siam. On the first day we lined Whitehall, the next day somewhere near the Mansion House. As we marched from Whitehall back to Horse Guards Parade on the first day we were caught in a thunderstorm; white blanco from our webbing made a mess of our uniforms. We noted with some satisfaction thet the Guards regiment had stopped to put on raincoats.

Trade training at RAF Freckleton was very relaxed after Bridgnorth. Like many National Servicemen we were allocated to trades that the regulars did not want, hence many of us finished up as 'medics' — Nursing Attendants oficially. I recall that there were too many airmen posted to Freckleton at that time, so I spent two weeks waiting for the course to start, but was able to visit Blackpool quite often.

Most of my service was spent at RAF Hornchurch, from November 1960 to April 1962. We were only required to be on camp during working hours and when we were 'on call', so this was a very relaxed RAF Station. One warm day I was cleaning the mortuary — which was never used while I was at Hornchurch — with the doors open. One of the civilian NAAFI ladies stopped her bicycle and came in. "What do you keep in here?" she asked, "I have never seen the doors open before". I said "It's the mortuary" and turned to switch off the water; when I turned back she and her bicycle had gone, very quickly!

During my last days at Hornchurch, all equipment and stores had to be transferred prior to closure of the Station. At the end it was found that we had a surplus 'display' Spitfire. It was a great joke at the time, but I often wondered what happened to that aircraft — what a price it would fetch today!

My last six weeks of service were spent at RAF Biggin Hill. Those who were transferred from Hornchurch thought that it should have remained open and Biggin Hill closed.

APPENDIX

A selection of ditties, two of which you may have heard before!

A National Service Airman Remembers

Just a letter through the posting flap
To land on passage floor,
A letter that would change my life
Came flutt'ring through the door.

A letter in buff envelope,
Complete with official stamp,
An invite from Her Majesty
To report to distant camp

A similar letter sent countrywide
To many a mother's son,
They travel both by train and bus
and meet at Cardington.

Now herded to the cookhouse for
A meal, or so we're told,
Of crispy bacon and square eggs,
With chips not far from cold.

Then marched down to the billet,
A wooden shed with beds,
You're told so much in such short time
There are many puzzled heads.

The escort guide has left us,
For this is now free time;
You talk and write a letter home
To say that all is fine.

Next day it's time for haircuts,
Short back and sides is best,
Then medicals and X-rays
And colour blindness test.

In an interview that follows
They assess your qualities,
You try to get into your trade
But will have to wait and see.

You're issued with a number
To remember all your days:
It's used throughout your service life
In many different ways.

We march down to the clothing store
For blues that may not fit,
With webbing, boots and eating tools
Plus the dreaded cleaning kit.

Back now to the billet,
Where demonstrations start
To show you how to do your kit
And get you dressed quite smart.

A week has passed — it's time to leave
On a train that's far from slow,
Your drill instructors you have met
For the trip to RAF Wilmslow.

We march from station to the camp,
The work has just begun
To turn us into airmen
There's lots more to be done.

The billets here, still wooden huts,
With highly polished floor,
To move around from place to place
We use pads found by the door.

A rota on the notice board
To tell us what to dust
We polish windows and the floor,
Each single task a must.

We're taught to march, to turn about,
Come smartly to the halt,
Sixty plus to act as one,
Without the slightest fault.

We graduate to arms drill,
The long rifles thrown about,
We struggle in the early days
While DIs rave and shout.

We march down for our needles,
Our arms they feel like lead,
But for us two hours of arms drill
While some should be in bed.

They make us sample tear gas,
An experience to be told,
For when it's ordered "Masks off"
Eyes stream, like full with cold.

There's also ground defence to learn,
With weapon training taught,
For when your camp is threatened
The intruders must be fought.

Five weeks have passed, relief at last,
The shoes and brasses gleam,
Our blues as well must look their best
For the snowdrops' looks are keen.

With great relief we pass the gate,
The first time off camp is fine,
Enjoy our freedom while we may
Make the most of precious time.

When introduced to R & I
We climb ropes over frozen pools;
A few succeed around the course,
Most fall and laugh like fools!

In trucks we head out for the hills
To spend time in tented camp,
Wash and shave in montain streams
While the dew's still thick and damp.

Here we build our bridges,
Sling ropes and make our swings,
The meals we cook, the canteens wash,
We survive through all those things.

In section strength we are sent out
O'er hills and down the hollow,
We read the maps and find the clues
Whose instructions we must follow.

The trail takes us some thirty miles
On tired and weary feet;
All are glad to see the end
In Buxton town's main street.

The time is close; rehearsals start
For Passing Out Parade;
We practice hard and give our all
With last adjustments made.

In we're marched and brought to Halt
On sacred drilling square
To face the officers and guests
With them our day to share.

We then march past in column
And review in open line,
The orders given sharp and clear;
To all it looks just fine.

Back now to the billet,
Sad times, for we must part,
The time has come to go on leave
Before trade training starts.

I've often wondered what became
Of those, my service mates,
I sometimes wish with some regret
We'd made a future date.

[Rhondda Boy]

We are the Royal Air Force

We are the Royal Air Force,
No bloody use are we,
The only time you see us
Is breakfast, lunch and tea.

But when our Country needs us
We'll shout with all our might
"Per Ardua Ad Astra,
**** you, Jack, I'm all right".

[Trad., to the tune 'The Church's One Foundation']

West Kirby

They say that West Kirby's a wonderful place,
But the organisation's a bloody disgrace.
We've Corporals and Sergeants and Flight Sergeants too,
With their hands in their pockets and nothing to do.

They stand on the square and they bawl and they shout
They shout about things they know sod all about.
For all that they've taught me I might as well be
Where the mountains of Mourne sweep down to the sea.

[Traditional]